THE
INNOCENT
DIVERSION

YOUNG LADY AT A CABINET PIANO FORTE (c. 1808)

PATRICK PIGGOTT

THE INNOCENT
DIVERSION

*A study of Music in
the life and writings of
Jane Austen*

DOUGLAS CLEVERDON
THE CLOVER HILL EDITIONS
LONDON 1979

The tenth of the Clover Hill Editions
Published by
DOUGLAS CLEVERDON
27 Barnsbury Square, London N.1

Printed at Skelton's Press
Wellingborough, Northants.

To
Isména Holland

CONTENTS

ACKNOWLEDGEMENTS

I am deeply indebted to the following:

The Jane Austen Memorial Trust for kind permission to study the collection of Music Books housed in the Jane Austen Memorial Trust Museum at Chawton and for allowing me to use two pages from these books as illustrations. Also to the Museum's curator, Mrs Elizabeth Rose, for her hospitality and ready welcome during my visits to Chawton.

Mr H. L. Jenkyns for allowing me to investigate the collection of Austen Music Books in his care (referred to hereinafter, at his request, as the Second Collection) which contains important volumes formerly belonging to Cassandra Austen and Mrs Henry Austen (née Hancock), and for supplying and permitting me to use as illustrations two pages from these books.

Mr V. J. Kite, Librarian for the Bath and Wansdyke Area of the County of Avon for permission to reproduce concert advertisements from the Bath Chronicle; also to the Bath Reference Library and its staff for much assistance during my researches into musical activities in late 18th and early 19th century Bath.

The British Museum, Department of Prints and Drawings for supplying and granting permission for the reproduction of the portraits of Mrs Billington and Signor Morelli.

The National Portrait Gallery for supplying and granting permission for the reproduction of the portrait by John Jackson of Catherine Stephens and the pencil sketch of Mrs Dickons.

S. E. H. Broadwood Esq., Managing Director of John Broadwood & Sons, Ltd., for details concerning the costs and transport of Broadwood pianos in the Regency period and for other information concerning Broadwood's business arrangements at that time.

Kalman A. Burnam, Chairman and Fletcher Professor of Drama, Tuft's University, Midford, Mass., for information about the Meyer and Weippart families of Harpists.

Adrian B. Rance of Winchester City Museum (Curator, Miss Elizabeth Lewis, B.A., A.M.A.) for supplying the portrait of Dr Chard and for kindly giving permission for its reproduction.

Kent County Library and its Divisional Librarian, Mr H. V. Ralph, A.L.A., for details of concert advertisements in the Kentish Gazette for 1811.

Mrs M. Legrand of Bath City Council Leisure and Tourist Services for information about the New Assembly Rooms, Bath.

Mr David Gilson for valuable introductions, and for his interest and encouragement.

Mrs Lorella Matthews for much important advice and for her stimulating interest in the subject of this study and the progress of my work.

Mr and Mrs Douglas Cleverdon for their unfailing encouragement and enthusiasm and for their scrupulous editing of my work.

For all quotations from Jane Austen's writings I have relied entirely on the late Dr R. W. Chapman's editions, published by the Oxford University Press, to which all page references refer.

APOLOGIA

THIS BOOK is for readers who share my own intense delight in Jane Austen's art. Other people, those to whom that art is mysteriously antipathetic (they really do exist, and they are more than Twain), and those, more to be pitied than censured, who find *Pride and Prejudice* enjoyable but can see little in the great writer's other works need not attempt to read it. In fact, they had better not read it, for I have indulged myself, not only with copious quotations from Jane Austen's writings, but with the frequent incorporation into my own text of idioms and phrases whose provenance will be immediately recognised by the thousands of her admirers who have her books by heart but may, perhaps, be overlooked by the rest of the reading public. My use of characteristic 'Austenisms' is, indeed, so considerable that I have not indicated their sources. Had I done so my modest book would have required a vast addition to its already sufficiently numerous footnotes.

Jane Austen once paraphrased for her sister's amusement some lines, faintly comic in themselves, from Walter Scott's *Marmion*:

> I do not rhyme to that dull elf
> Who cannot image to himself

When writing to Cassandra, *à propos* the publication of *Pride and Prejudice*, she concluded a paragraph in her letter thus:

> I do not write for such dull elves
> As have not a great deal of imagination themselves

and I, in my turn, am tempted to expand her sly parody of Scott, for

> I do not write for such dull elves
> As have not, in the course of reading Jane Austen's novels over and over again, so committed them to memory that they can have no difficulty in recognising quotations from them for themselves.

'I consider music as a very innocent diversion, and perfectly compatible with the profession of a clergyman.'

MR COLLINS (*Pride and Prejudice.* p. 101)

CHAPTER I

'Do Not Expect a Prodigy'

JANE AUSTEN was musical: she played the pianoforte. Though by no means an outstanding performer she must have played, in the common phrase, 'well enough'; well enough, that is, for her own and her family's entertainment in their leisure hours, and certainly well enough to please her young friends and relations with cotillions and quadrilles (like her own Mrs Weston, who was so 'capital in her country dances') whenever they found themselves sufficiently numerous to make up a set,[1] which must have happened with increasing frequency as her brothers' families grew ever larger.

Music in the England of Jane Austen's time, and for long afterwards, was an essential part of a young lady's education. It had a special role in the social life of the day, particularly for that part of the population, much the larger, which did not live in London, Bath, or one of the few other places where public performances by professionals might be heard. For music, next to dancing (though dancing could not be enjoyed without music), was the favourite amusement of most young people, and any lady who played was sure to have her share of attention, admiration and gratitude. The importance of music and amateur music-making in the plots and characterisation of Jane Austen's novels is, therefore, considerable. Her girls are nearly all musical; only Catherine Morland, as a small girl, tries but fails to learn the pianoforte, and even she is eventually able to 'listen to other people's performance with very little fatigue'; while Fanny Price,

with her hypersensitive feelings and introverted tempera-
ment, would undoubtedly have found in music a solace
and a much-needed form of self-expression had she been
given the same opportunities as her rich cousins, the
Bertram sisters. Elinor Dashwood, so accomplished with
the pencil and the paintbrush, probably did begin to learn
music in her childhood, but had to give it up when her
sister Marianne, with characteristic blindness to other
people's feelings, monopolised the family instrument to
such an extent that it was eventually regarded as her own
property. It is a mystery how the youngest Dashwood
sister, Margaret, ever contrived to practise at all, with
Marianne playing and singing all day long, and I have a
suspicion that the principal among Mrs Dashwood's
reasons – though she will not have admitted it, even to
herself – for being so ready to allow her two elder daughters to go to London for a long visit to vulgar, good-natured
Mrs Jennings, was the vexed question of Margaret's
musical education:

> 'Margaret and I shall be as much benefited by it as
> yourselves . . . we shall go on so quietly and happily
> together with our books and our music!'
>
> (Sense and Sensibility, p. 155)

Most of the other Austen heroines and anti-heroines
play. Some of them play really well – Jane Fairfax
brilliantly, with Anne Elliot and Mary Crawford not far
behind. Elizabeth Bennet, Emma Woodhouse, Caroline
Bingley and the Bertram sisters all play, 'well enough'
(about as well, one supposes, as Jane Austen herself),
and their playing, and sometimes even their instruments,
are skilfully woven into the stories of their joys and
sorrows. We may be sure that Jane Austen would not
have made such liberal use of music in her work if it had
not been a very noticeable feature of her world, for few
important writers have recorded with a more scrupulous
accuracy the manners and tastes of the middle classes of
their time. Though her art, like that of many other great

novelists, still finds occasional depreciators, amid an infinity of admirers, there is a pretty general agreement that the historical truth of her account of life as it was lived in Regency England cannot be questioned.

The men in Jane Austen's novels do not play, or if they do they keep quiet about it. They sometimes sing, but their function in relation to music is not to perform but to listen to and admire the musical talents of the opposite sex. Spinster though she was, Jane Austen, through her brothers, knew a great deal about the lives of men, and since practically all those in her own circle who did not belong to the top-most stratum of middle-class society – the landowners – followed one of the only three professions which were completely acceptable to her class – the army, the navy and the church – it is natural that the men in her books should do the same. It is true that we also meet there a few who are 'in the law line', but although the Ferrars family 'allowed the law to be genteel enough', and in spite of John Knightley's relatively superior status as the younger brother of a landed proprietor, a lawyer's social position in the first decades of the nineteenth century was still in a state of flux. The sycophantic attorney, Mr Shepherd, is only tolerated by Sir Walter Elliot because of his usefulness as a general factotum, and it is perhaps significant that it is Mr Shepherd's daughter, Mrs Clay (symbolic name!), who is cast by her creator for the role of the one scheming and unprincipled adventuress in all the six novels.

To be 'in trade' was, of course, to be beyond the middle-class pale, and perhaps the reason for a few light but surprising touches of vulgarity about the otherwise delightful Elizabeth Bennet ('There is a fine old English saying ... "keep your breath to cool your porridge" ') can be traced to her mother's socially inferior family. For even Mr Gardiner, Mrs Bennet's brother, who has quite 'the air of a gentleman', is, unfortunately, 'in trade' and therefore only 'moderately genteel'. Indeed, it is one of the signs of Mr Darcy's 'reformation' that, to Elizabeth's great surprise, he accepts, without reservation, the Gardiners, her favourite aunt and uncle, as his equals, in spite of their residence near their warehouses in Cheapside.

What Jane Austen might have made of a hero or a villain who practised one of the arts as a profession we can only conjecture, for she lived at a time when even poets and painters, unless of strictly amateur status, were still precariously poised on the very fringe of respectability, while it was much too early for a mere musician to be tolerated as a romantic figure. We have only to recall the extraordinary commotion caused in London literary circles by the decision of Dr Johnson's friend, Mrs Thrale, a brewer's widow, to marry an Italian singing master, Signor Piozzi, and the Jove-like denunciations of her action by the outraged Doctor (admittedly he had been thinking of marrying her himself), to realise that musicians in the late eighteenth century were liable to be classed with apothecaries and governesses as beings of an altogether inferior order. Mrs Thrale's '*mésalliance*' occurred during Jane Austen's childhood, but that she herself, twenty years later, possessed a somewhat Johnsonian opinion of professional musicians is clear enough from a passage in a letter to her sister Cassandra, written in 1815:

> The truth is I think, that they are all, at least Music Masters, made of too much consequence & allowed to take too many Liberties with their Scholar's time.
>
> (*Letters*, p. 440)

and she also reported that the hired performers at a private concert which she attended in 1811:

> gave great satisfaction by doing what they were paid for, & giving themselves no airs.
>
> (*Letters*, p. 274)

Jane Austen encountered very few professional artists of any kind and she never met a musical genius. It would, therefore, have been a transgression of her self-imposed limits had she ever attempted to portray such a person in any of her novels. The arts were, naturally, of importance to her, but, with the exception of literature, she valued them principally as an essential part of a good general education. They might be acquired by anyone who could afford 'the benefit of masters'. With the lives and artistic achievements of the masters themselves she was not concerned; her interest, as a novelist, was in the effect of their teaching on the characters and fortunes of their pupils.

Jane Austen knew a good deal about the graphic arts, and, as Dr Frank Bradbrook has brilliantly demonstrated,[2] she not only read and approved William Gilpin's various writings on 'The Picturesque', but allowed them to have an important influence on her work. Familiarity with the technical language of drawing is made manifest in the Tilneys' discussion of the subject in *Northanger Abbey*, and, more amusingly, by Mr Elton's misuse of some of its terminology in *Emma*; and Jane Austen is said to have been no mean performer with the pencil herself.[3] But a competence in drawing was not her main artistic 'acquirement', for she was for long the principal, if not the only musician in her family circle.

When Jane Austen first began to learn music is not known, but she probably had pianoforte lessons during her years at school, which lasted, on and off, from 1782 until 1787. That she was still studying under a master as late as 1796, in her 21st year, we have evidence in a letter written to her sister in September of that year:

> I am glad to hear so good an account of Mr Charde, and only fear that my long absence may occasion his relapse. I practise every day as much as I can – I wish it were more for his sake.
>
> (*Letters*, p. 10)

George William Chard (the additional 'e' seems to have been a slip of Jane Austen's pen) was, in 1796, assistant organist and a lay-clerk at Winchester Cathedral, of which he became organist six years later (*Plate* I). Jane Austen was lucky in her teacher, for Mr (later Dr) Chard was an extremely good musician: an excellent organist, a composer and, at least in his earlier years, a teacher with a sense of vocation. He was to earn a modest fame as a trainer of boys' voices, and eventually became 'The Master of the Music' at Winchester College. In 1796 he would have been obliged to supplement his salary by a good deal of private teaching, and it is significant that he was prepared to travel approximately fourteen miles from Winchester to Steventon to give Miss Jane Austen music lessons, though he probably had a whole round of pupils to visit on the same day, for it must be understood that it was the custom then, and for long afterwards, for music teachers to give their lessons at their pupils' homes.[4]

Jane Austen sang a little, as well as played. We know, on the authority of her nephew, J. E. Austen-Leigh, that she possessed 'a small, but sweet voice'. Furthermore, her exquisitely hand-written music books contain almost as many simple songs as pianoforte solos and duets. Certainly in Mr Chard she had a master who was well able to develop such small vocal talent as she may have possessed, but her voice was probably never anything remarkable or we should have heard more about it, and as she confessed to taking little pleasure in the singing of others, however excellent, it is unlikely that she persevered for long with her own. But her playing was another matter, for she found recreation, and perhaps even inspiration, in her regular early-morning practice hour, which in her later years seems to have been almost the only part of the day when she could be sure of remaining quite undisturbed. Like her own Anne Elliot, she probably developed an ability to lose herself in thought 'while her fingers were mechanically at work, proceeding for half an hour together, equally without error and without consciousness', and this faculty, though it can scarcely have promoted her musical development, at least kept her fingers supple and ready for the lively dance music which she was always happy to play for the amusement of her nephews and nieces.

It is an awkward circumstance that a writer who not only played herself but made as frequent use as did Jane Austen of music and amateur musicians in her novels should have owned to a decidedly ambivalent attitude to the musical performances of other people. She quite liked listening to the pianoforte or the harp (though not to singing) in the drawing-rooms of friends and relations, but public concerts seem to have bored her and her one recorded visit to the opera proved a very decided failure. But before we begin to be severe on her for the disconcertingly philistine remarks she sometimes made about music it will be as well to try to discover what we can about the concerts she actually attended.

ILLUSTRATIONS

Frontispiece:

YOUNG LADY AT A CABINET PIANO FORTE (c. 1808). The instrument is an example of the fashionable but short-lived Cabinet Piano Forte, soon to be superseded by the lower and therefore more practical Upright Pianoforte, from which today's instruments are descended. The engraving was found in an old copy of J. B. Cramer's *Instructions for the Piano Forte*.

I   WILLIAM CHARD, Jane Austen's music master. This unsigned portrait is thought to have been painted in 1792 when Chard was on a visit to Bath.

II   SYDNEY-GARDEN VAUXHALL, BATH. Advertisement in the *Bath Chronicle* of May 30th, 1799, for a Grand Gala and open-air concert, which Jane Austen attended on June 4th.

III   NEW ASSEMBLY-ROOMS, BATH. Advertisement in the *Bath Chronicle* of April 4th, 1805 for a Subscription Concert on April 17th. On this occasion the Austen family, minus Cassandra, heard Mrs Billington, Giovanni Morelli and other singers, as well as a full programme of orchestral music.

IV   MRS BILLINGTON (1768–1818) in the character of St Cecilia. Engraving by A. Cardon after the painting by Sir Joshua Reynolds.

V   GIOVANNI MORELLI, the popular bass singer who took part in Rauzzini's Benefit Concert on April 17th, 1805.

VI   MARIA DICKONS (c. 1770–1833) as the Countess in Mozart's *The Marriage of Figaro*, a role which she sang at the first English performance of the opera in June, 1812. Jane Austen heard her sing in Canterbury in 1813.

VII   CATHERINE STEPHENS (1794–1882). From a portrait by John Jackson in the National Portrait Gallery. Jane Austen heard her sing the part of Mandane in Arne's *Artaxerxes* in 1814, and considered that she had 'a pleasing person'. In 1839 she married the octogenarian Earl of Essex, who died a year later.

VIII   'STRIKE THE HARP'. Part of Eliza Austen's manuscript copy of Bishop's three-part glee, 'Strike the harp in praise of Bragela'. The accompaniment is for pianoforte, four hands. This glee is mentioned by Jane Austen in her account of the Henry Austens' musical party at their Sloane Street house in 1811; she quotes it in Austen-family nonsense language as 'Poike per parp pin Praise pof Prepala'.

IX-XII See pp. 132-6

I   WILLIAM CHARD

SYDNEY-GARDEN VAUXHALL,

THE MOST SPACIOUS AND BEAUTIFUL PUBLICK GARDEN IN THE KINGDOM.

ON TUESDAY next the FOURTH of JUNE,
THERE WILL BE

A GRAND GALA,

In Honour of his MAJESTY's BIRTH-DAY,
In a Stile of Magnificence never exceeded.

The Evening's Entertainment will confist of a
Concert of Vocal & Instrumental Music,
IN THE NEW ORCHESTRA;
In the courfe of which, Mr. NIMROIDE will give his
wonderful IMITATIONS of the BIRDS.

Principal Inftrumental Performers,
Leader of the Band, Mr. Richards; Violoncello, Mr.
Herfchell; Oboe, Mr. Affley.

Principal Vocal Performers,

| Mr. TAYLOR, | Mafter GRAY, |
| Mr. SHEPHERD, | Mifs RICHARDSON. |

Act I. Overture, Haydn. Song, Mr. Shepherd.
Glee, Meffrs. Cook, Shell, Shepherd, and Taylor. Song,
Mifs Richardfon, Nightingale. Glee. Song, Mafter
Gray. Song, Mr. Taylor.

Act II. Overture, Pleyel. Song, Mafter Gray. Glee.
Comic Song, Mr. Taylor. Glee. Song, Mifs Richardfon. Duet. Full Piece.

Act III. Overture, Haydn. *Mr. Nimroide's Imitations.*
Comic Song, Mr. Taylor. Song, Mafter Gray. To
conclude with " God fave the King," in Full Chorus.

Between the 2d and 3d Acts of the Concert,
THERE WILL BE A MOST

CAPITAL DISPLAY OF FIRE-WORKS,

By Signor INVETTO,
Who will exert the utmoft of his ingenious ftile to
produce new and aftonifhing effects.
The ILLUMINATIONS will be moft BRILLIANT,
feveral new Devices and Decorations being prepared.

*Supper Parties well accommodated; many Rooms will be
open for that purpofe, and fufficient attendants engaged. Every
kind of Refreshment will be charged as reasonable as poffible.*

Tickets 2s. each, to be had at the Gate of the Garden;
at the White-Lion Inn; Mr. Kemp's grocery warehoufe,
Market-place; and at Meyler's library, in the Grove.

Doors to be open at Five, and the Concert to begin
at Seven o'clock.——Admiffion 2s. each.

☞ The next PUBLIC BREAKFAST will be on
MONDAY the 3d of JUNE, attended with Horns,
Clarionets, &c. [3734

II   SYDNEY-GARDEN VAUXHALL, BATH

NEW ASSEMBLY-ROOMS.

M R. RAUZZINI most respectfully acquaints
the Nobility, Gentry, and the Public in general,
that on WEDNESDAY April 17th, 1805, there will be

A SUBSCRIPTION CONCERT,

For his SPRING BENEFIT.

PRINCIPAL VOCAL PERFORMERS,

MRS. BILLINGTON,

MISS SHARP, and SIGNOR MORELLI.

GLEE PERFORMERS,

Messrs. COOKE, ASHLEY, GRAY, and DOYLE.

Mr. BINGER will play a Concerto on the Violin.

Principal Instrumental Performers,

First Violin,	Mr. Richards	Oboe,	Mr. Ashley
Violoncello,	Mr. Herschell	Flute,	Mr. Stainsbury
Bassoon,	Mr. J. Ashley	Trumpet,	Mr. Waite.

Subscriptions received at the Rooms only——THREE
TICKETS for ONE GUINEA.

Admittance to Non-Subscribers, HALF-A-GUINEA.

Non-Subscribers' Tickets to be had of Mr. RAUZZINI,
Queen-square; Messrs. Linterns', church-yard; Mr. Ash-
ley, Wade's-passage; Mr. Philpot, Bennet-street; and at
the Rooms.

N.B. Those Ladies and Gentlemen who intend sub-
scribing, are most respectfully acquainted, that their
Tickets will be ready for delivery on *Saturday April 13th,*
and to prevent any confusion, the Subscription will close
on *Tuesday Evening April 16th,* as none but Non-Subscribers' Tickets can be delivered on the day of performance.

*Those Ladies and Gentlemen who wish to sit in the Gallery,
are respectfully informed that it is fitted up for their reception.*

To begin at Half-past Seven o'clock.

Mr. RAUZZINI most respectfully informs the Subscri-
bers and the Public, that none will be admitted at the re-
hearsal.——Further particulars will be given in the Bills.

III   NEW ASSEMBLY-ROOMS, BATH

Mrs Billington
in the character of
St CECILIA,

Engraven by Mr Cardon from the original Picture
by Sir Joshua Reynolds.

Published by John Bell, Southampton Street, Strand, May 1st 1812.

IV   MRS BILLINGTON (1768–1818)

The Celebrated

SIGNOR MORELLI.

Febo gli diè di chiara voce il vanto,

Euterpe gl'ispirò l'arte del canto,

Talia mostrogli il gesto, ond'ebbe Laude:

Europa tutta ascolta, osserva, e applaude.

London, Published as the Act directs April 18th. 1797. by P. Molinari N°. 72 New Compton Street, Soho.

V   GIOVANNI MORELLI

VI   MARIA DICKONS (C. 1770–1833)

VII   CATHERINE STEPHENS (1794–1882)

VIII   'STRIKE THE HARP'

CHAPTER II

Public and Private Music-Making

PUBLIC CONCERTS in Jane Austen's time were rare events outside London or Bath. She may have heard a certain amount of music in Winchester or Basingstoke during her Steventon girlhood (though there is no evidence that she did), but the first concert mentioned in her letters was no more than an open-air performance, with 'illuminations' and fireworks, given in Sydney Gardens, Bath, on June 4th, 1799 (*Plate* II). It appears, however, that she must already have been present at a similar entertainment elsewhere, since she anticipated that

> . . . the Concert will have more than it's usual charm with me, as the gardens are large enough for me to get pretty well beyond the reach of its sound.
>
> (*Letters*, p. 65)

This cannot be passed over as a case of distance literally lending enchantment, for she obviously did not really want to hear the music at all. However, such music as was played *en plein air* in late eighteenth century Bath was not often of much consequence. At the weekly 'public teas' in Sydney Gardens a background of light music was usually provided by a band consisting of a few horns and 'clarionets', and if Jane Austen could have expected to hear no more than this we might be indulgent to her over her lack of interest in it and her evident preference for the fireworks and 'illuminations'. But the 'Grand Gala Concert' given that fourth of June in what the *Bath Chronicle*

17

described as 'the most spacious and beautiful publick garden in the kingdom', was an event of a superior order. It was planned as a celebration of King George III's birthday, and it promised to be 'In a Stile of Magnificence never exceeded'. The advertisement of it in the *Bath Chronicle*'s issue of May 30th stated that the evening's entertainment would consist of a concert of vocal and instrumental music 'In the course of which, Mr NIMROIDE will give his wonderful IMITATIONS OF BIRDS.' Mr Nimroide was, obviously, a sop to public taste, but the music performed was nicely suited to the occasion. Apart from three Overtures, two by Haydn and one by his pupil Pleyel, (all three probably what we would now call symphonies), the programme was exclusively vocal. There were numerous songs, some serious and some comic; a duet; four glees; and finally the whole affair was rounded off with 'God Save the King', sung in 'Full Chorus'. But if Jane Austen had really carried out her stated intention, she would have heard very little of all this, for she would have quietly wandered out of earshot of it and sought a strategic position where she might, while still taking advantage of the excellent catering arrangements ('Every kind of Refreshment will be charged as reasonable as possible'), command a good view of the 'CAPITAL DISPLAY OF FIREWORKS by Signor INVETTO' which was advertised to take place in the interval between the second and third 'Acts' of the concert. Unfortunately the firework display had to be abandoned because of unfavourable weather conditions and this caused such general disappointment that it was decided to repeat the whole of the Grand Gala on the evening of June 18th. Jane Austen and her party ventured once more to Sydney Gardens, and though they arrived too late to hear most of the music (probably by design) they were

> in very good time for the Fire-works, which were really beautiful, & surpassing my expection; – the illuminations too were very pretty.

(*Letters*, p. 71)

From 1801 to June, 1806, Jane Austen was actually resident in Bath. During five winters, therefore, she had plenty of opportunity to hear really good music. On Wednesday evenings throughout the season subscription concerts took place at the New Assembly Rooms under the direction of the celebrated Signor Rauzzini, and though she may not have been a regular supporter of these concerts she was certainly present at some of them. For Rauzzini's Subscription Concerts were an essential part of Bath's social life, along with the balls, the theatre and morning visits to the Pump Room. Furthermore, one of the most important scenes in *Persuasion* takes place at a Bath concert, and it gives the reader a vivid impression of the brilliance of such occasions. It tells us, indeed, rather more about them than Jane Austen's account of an actual concert which she attended on April 17th, 1805 (*Plate* III). Writing to her sister of that event, she had nothing at all to say about the music, mentioning only that

> you were very right in supposing that I wore my crape
> sleeves to the concert, I had them put in on the occasion.
> (*Letters*, p. 154)

and we hear no more of the evening's entertainment except that a Mr and Miss Bendish joined the Austens' party during the course of it. We can, however, discover from the *Bath Chronicle* of April 4th that the music Jane Austen heard (and, it must be feared, failed to appreciate) included a 'Military Overture' by Haydn (likely to be the work we now know as the 'Military' Symphony, No. 100, in G); the 'Overture in *Ariadne*' (composer unnamed);[5] an 'Overture' by Mozart (almost certainly another symphony); a violin concerto played by a Mr Singer; and the usual abundance of vocal music: arias, duets, trios, glees, etc. The vocalists included several of Rauzzini's 'regulars', who acted as supporting artists at most of his concerts, among them a still popular, if now somewhat *passé* Italian basso, Giovanni Morelli (*Plate* V), a favourite

with the British public for many years. Morelli's origins
were extremely humble: from being a mere 'running-
footman' to Lord Cowper, an English grandee travelling
in Italy, he had risen to the position of first *buffo caricato*
at London's celebrated King's Theatre. But by 1805, with
his vocal powers diminished, he had to give place to a
more famous singer, the great coloratura soprano, Mrs
Billington (*Plate* IV), who, as Rauzzini's advertisement
in the Bath paper makes clear, was the 'star' of the
occasion. It really is extraordinary that Jane Austen
should have had absolutely nothing to tell her sister
about this celebrity, who was known and admired
throughout Europe.

Elizabeth Billington was about thirty-seven in 1805,
and she was at the height of her powers. Though not
primarily a dramatic or a 'pathetic' singer, she was unsurpassed for the purity of her tone and the brilliance of
her technique. Among the items she chose for her Bath
appearance was one of her *pièces de résistance*: an *aria
bravura*, with obbligato parts for violin, 'cello and oboe,
from J. C. Bach's opera, *La Clemenza di Scipione*, and it is
with some effort that one is able to forgive Jane Austen
for remaining silent about it. Dr Chapman has hinted
that the rather trivial subject matter of some of Jane
Austen's letters to her sister reflects Cassandra's taste rather
than her own; that Cassandra preferred gossip about
friends and details of the latest fashions to the discussion
of weightier matters, and that Jane obliged accordingly.[6]
Be this as it may (and who can disprove it?), it is not a little
disconcerting to find Jane Austen writing, almost in the
style of Isabella Thorpe ('Anne Mitchell had tried to put
on a turban like mine, as I wore it the week before at the
concert'), about her 'crape sleeves' rather than about the
genius of the great Mrs Billington.

Another letter to Cassandra, written from Godmersham
Park, her brother Edward's estate in Kent, on November
3rd, 1813, promises an account of a concert which was to
take place in Canterbury two days later; but when Jane

Austen wrote after the event she again passed over the
music she had heard without comment. One might have
supposed that, having laid out seven shillings on her ticket
(by no means a trifling sum in those days for a person of
very limited means), she would have expected a modicum
of artistic enjoyment. She must have known something of
the programme she would hear, for the concert promoter,
a Mr Saffery, had advertised its main attractions in the
Kentish Gazette for November 2nd. Principal among
these was the promised appearance of another popular
singer, Mrs Dickons (*Plate* VI), who had lately enhanced
her already distinguished reputation by singing the role
of the Countess in the first London performances of
Mozart's opera, *The Marriage of Figaro*. Mrs Dickons was
to be heard in several favourite songs, among them Daniel
Purcell's 'Mad Bess' and the aria, 'Oh Ye Priests', from
Handel's oratorio, *Jephtha*, and there were to be choral
selections from Haydn's *Creation*. But one has an uneasy
feeling that Jane Austen regarded concerts of this type as
purely social events at which she could enjoy a 'comfort-
able coze' with old friends – and not merely during the
intervals between the 'Acts', for it must not be supposed
that a close attention to the efforts of the musicians was
considered absolutely necessary at concerts in Jane
Austen's time; on the contrary, matters were often quite
otherwise. Certainly, although she apparently remained
indifferent to Mrs Dickons and the other performers, Jane
Austen had plenty to report of the company she met at the
concert, and she made particular mention of a Lady B.
(Lady Bridges, mother-in-law of her brother Edward), who
earned her approbation 'for being in a hurry to have the
concert over & get away.' Indeed, a certain indifference
to music sometimes appears to have been a positive
recommendation to her, for we find a Miss Holder, whom
it was 'the fashion ... to think very detestable', proving on
acquaintance to be better than report, 'especially as Miss
Holder owns that she has no taste for music'. Jane Austen
is, of course, laughing at herself as well as at poor Miss

Holder, but there is more than a grain of truth intermixed
with her nonsense.

Not that she was always an unwilling or an entirely
uninterested listener. Her brother Henry and his wife
gave a grand musical party during a visit which she paid
to them in London in 1811, and she looked forward to it
with something very like excitement:

> above 80 people are invited for next tuesday Eveng &
> there is to be some very good Music, 5 professionals, 3
> of them Glee singers, besides Amateurs . . . One of the
> Hirelings, is a Capital on the Harp, from which I expect
> great pleasure.
>
> (*Letters*, pp. 269, 270)

Hirelings indeed! Still, we know now that she could enjoy the sound of good harp-playing, and in her next letter
she regaled Cassandra with a full account of the programme:

> The Music was extremely good. It opened. . . . with
> 'Poike pe parp pin Praise pof Prepala' [this, it appears,
> was Austen-family nonsense language for 'Strike the
> Harp in praise of Bragela': *Plate* VIII] & of the other
> Glees I remember, 'In Peace Love tunes,' 'Rosabelle,'
> 'The Red Cross Knight,' & 'Poor Insect.' Between the
> Songs were Lessons on the Harp, or Harp and Piano
> Forte together,[7] – & the Harp Player was Wiepart,
> whose name seems famous, tho' new to me.[8] – There
> was one female singer, a short Miss Davis all in blue,
> bringing up for the Public Line, whose voice was said
> to be very fine indeed.
>
> (*Letters*, p. 274)

It will be noted that Jane Austen gives only the general
opinion of short Miss Davis's singing: she was not prepared to praise it herself.

Perhaps it was as well that no amateurs were brave
enough to 'exhibit' at the Henry Austens' party, for the
programme must have been quite long enough without
them. It had been hoped that a certain Comte

D'Antraigues (Jane Austen spells his name D'Entraigues)
and his son, 'Count' Julien, would be among the guests,
for the son was known to be a very 'superior' performer,
presumably on the pianoforte. In the event, the
D'Antraigues were otherwise engaged, but the invitation
resulted in a visit by the entire Austen party to the Comte's
home, where they admired his collection of valuable
pictures and had an opportunity of hearing 'Count'
Julien. Jane Austen found his performance 'very wonderful'. Mrs Henry Austen, formerly the Comtesse de Feullide
(her first husband had met his death by the guillotine in
1794), evidently retained links with the French emigré
circles in London to which the D'Antraigues also belonged.
She can have had no inkling that the Comte was not all he
seemed to be; that he was in fact a very doubtful character. For many years he had worked as a secret agent, or,
rather, as a double secret agent, acting in turn (and sometimes even simultaneously) for France, Prussia and Russia,
and though he had been clever enough to survive for a
long time in this most dangerous of professions he had
finally been forced to flee from his headquarters in
Dresden and had arrived, in 1806, in England, armed with
letters of introduction which purported to be from no less
a personage than the Emperor of Russia (the Comte was,
incidentally, an expert forger). Despite the apparently
peaceful retirement in which he was living at the time of
the Austens' visit, Comte D'Antraigues was probably still
engaged in hazardous enterprises, for he came to a violent
end a few months later, stabbed to death by an Italian
manservant.[9]

Before she concluded the letter which gave Cassandra
an account of their sister-in-law's party, Jane Austen
threw in the following 'musical' character sketch of their
niece, Anna, the wayward, impulsive daughter of James
Austen, the incumbent of Steventon in succession to their
father:

She is quite an Anna with variations – but she cannot
have reached her last, for that is always the most

flourishing & shewey – she is at about her 3rd or 4th which are generally simple & pretty.

(Letters, p. 275)

This amused and amusing description of Anna was probably suggested to her aunt by the unusually large amount of music surrounding Jane Austen during that visit to London, and it is safe to assume that at least one of the 'Lessons' for harp played at Mrs Austen's party was in the form of a set of variations by some such celebrated harp composer of the day as Krumpholtz, Boscha, Naderman or de Marin. In all such display pieces the final variation is invariably 'flourishing' and 'shewey'.

We owe our detailed knowledge of Jane Austen's visits to London to the fact that when she was parted from Cassandra (they were rarely in London together) they corresponded regularly and at length, and Jane Austen was in London fairly frequently while her brother Henry lived there. Henry Austen – kind, affectionate and extremely proud of his brilliantly gifted sister – made every effort to entertain her while she was his guest. He took her to visit his friends in the city and the suburbs; they went driving in the parks; they visited exhibitions, and they frequently went to the theatre, where they saw, as well as various Shakespearean productions (though probably only in Garrick's so-called 'acting' versions of the plays), several rather more frivolous entertainments – comedies, farces, pantomines, and the occasional musical play, such as Dibdin's *The Farmer's Wife*. And once they went to the opera. Privately, Jane Austen did not at all relish the idea of an evening largely devoted to singing, though we may be sure that she was careful not to say so in case she spoiled the pleasure of her companions. She confided to Cassandra that,

> Excepting Miss Stephens, I daresay Artaxerxes will be very tiresome   (*Letters*, p. 384)

and in the event even the vocal charms of Miss Stephens left her cold:

Fanny and Mr J.P. are delighted with Miss S, & her merit in singing is I daresay very great; that she gave *me* no pleasure is no reflection upon her, nor I hope upon myself, being what Nature made me on that article. All I am sensible of in Miss S. is, a pleasing person & no skill in acting.

(*Letters*, p. 385)

Jane Austen was certainly right in her low estimation of Miss Stephens's acting, for Sir Henry Hadow fully confirms her opinion with his statement that 'she somewhat lacked dramatic instinct and her enunciation was very bad',[10] a criticism that could, alas, be levelled at many later divas, including large numbers of those at present before the public. Nevertheless, Catherine Stephens (*Plate* VII) was evidently a delightful singer. After a successful first appearance in 1812 at the Pantheon, an enormous building which provided Londoners with a wide variety of entertainments from 1770 until the ultimate failure of the enterprise in 1814 (among her fellow artists on the occasion was Giovanni Morelli, now almost voiceless but still kindly received for his acting ability), she made a sensational Covent Garden début in September, 1813, as Mandane in Thomas Arne's *Artaxerxes*,[11] and it was still the smart thing in March, 1814, to hear the new 'nightingale' in the opera which had launched her on her career – a career which was to continue with ever-increasing éclat until her retirement in 1835.[12] But for all Miss Stephens's 'pleasing person' and her extraordinary vocal attainments she found no favour with Jane Austen, who, being 'as nature made her' on the subject of singing, was satisfied that *she* was not at fault. Or so she may have thought until she met Charles Haden.

CHAPTER III

'Something between a Man and an Angel'

JANE AUSTEN met Mr Haden in the autumn of 1815 when she was staying at Henry's London house in Hans Place and nursing her brother through a serious illness. Henry's wife, Eliza had died in April, 1813, and Jane found him in the care of a young surgeon who, from the first, impressed her as very clever and attentive. Though she referred to him in a letter written on October 17th as 'the apothecary from the corner of Sloane Street', she was soon so charmed by his intelligence and good manners that she was concerned to do away any ideas her family in Chawton may have received that Mr Haden, as a mere apothecary, was 'not quite the thing'. Writing to Cassandra on December 2nd she allowed her wit full play as she set about correcting the impression she had herself created by her earlier mention of Mr Haden:

> . . . you seem to be under a mistake as to Mr H. – You call him an Apothecary; he is no Apothecary, he has never been an Apothecary, there is not an Apothecary in this Neighbourhood – the only inconvenience of the situation perhaps, but so it is – we have not a medical Man within reach – he is a Haden, nothing but a Haden, a sort of wonderful nondescript Creature on two legs, something between a Man & an Angel – but without the least spice of an Apothecary. – He is perhaps the only Person *not* an Apothecary hereabouts. – He has never sung to us. He will not sing without a P.Forté accompaniment.

> (*Letters*, pp. 439–440)

Charles Thomas Haden was indeed no ordinary apothecary. He was to become an ornament to the medical profession and to make several valuable contributions to it.[13] Jane Austen and her niece, Fanny, her brother Edward's eldest daughter, who had joined her in Hans Place as Henry's illness grew more alarming, were soon entirely charmed by Mr Haden. Fanny, who already played the pianoforte and was learning the harp, was evidently quite smitten, and perhaps Aunt Jane herself, despite her forty years and her confirmed spinsterhood, was a little in danger. Certainly aunt and niece were both agreeably fluttered when, as happened with increasing frequency, the young man's professional visits were extended to include the dinner hour and the subsequent music-making and conversation.

Mr Haden, as will have been noted, was musical. He was clearly known to be a singer, though he declined to sing without a pianoforte accompaniment (was he asked to sing unaccompanied or did Fanny proffer her services at the harp?). He was evidently an example of that extraordinarily intense passion for music which frequently possesses the members of the medical fraternity. Obviously he must have expatiated at length on his favourite subject (echoed and encouraged, no doubt, by Fanny), and perhaps he eventually raised in Jane Austen some sort of mild opposition. If so, he quite floored her with what appears to have been a quotation, or at least a paraphrase of those famous lines from *The Merchant of Venice*:

> The man that hath no music in himself,
> Nor is not moved with concord of sweet sounds,
> Is fit for treasons, strategems and spoils.

Jane Austen was obviously taken aback, and she does not seem to have realised that Mr Haden's outburst emanated from Shakespeare. In a letter to Cassandra of November 24th, 1815, she wrote:

> I have been listening to dreadful Insanity. – It is Mr Haden's firm opinion that a person *not* musical is fit for

every sort of wickedness. I ventured to assert a little on
the other side, but wished the cause in abler hands.

(Letters, p. 435)

The two younger members of the party were, it seems
clear, becoming attracted to one another. Does one detect
a faint note of unease in Jane Austen's hints to Cassandra
of a growing liking of Charles for Fanny, whose ability to
charm masculine susceptibilities with performances on
'a harp as elegant as herself' brings to mind Mary
Crawford?

> . . . then came the dinner & Mr Haden who brought
> good Manners & clever conversation; – from 7 to 8 the
> Harp; at 8 Mrs. L. & Miss E. arrived – & for the rest
> of the eveng. the Drawg. -room was thus arranged,
> on the Sopha-side the two ladies Henry & myself
> making the best of it, on the opposite side Fanny & Mr
> Haden in two chairs (I *believe* at least they had *two*
> chairs) talking together uninterruptedly.

(Letters, p. 437)

But whatever may have been the emotional disturbances
caused in the heart of the niece, and perhaps also in that
of the aunt, they were to subside as quickly as they arose.
Henry recovered, and the time came for Jane Austen to
return to Chawton. Mr Haden had lent her a few books –
she returned them with a note in which she expressed the
hope that he would call that evening at Hans Place –
'I leave town on Saturday & must say "Good bye" to
you'. As for Fanny's little flirtation, if such it was, it was
forgotten soon enough, for all her scribblings in her diary
about 'delightful, clever, musical Haden'.[14] Perhaps Mr
Haden was, after all, never much more to her than 'the
apothecary from the corner of Sloane Street', and therefore only to be ranked among the 'half-gentlemen'.

It was while Jane Austen was in London, nursing Henry
back to health, that another of her nieces, Caroline Austen,
Anna's younger sister, then aged ten, was sent to Chawton
to keep her grandmother and Aunt Cassandra company.
Caroline was learning to play the pianoforte: so she was

allowed to practise on her Aunt Jane's instrument. Its
owner charged her to

> ... practise your Music of course, & I trust to you for
> taking care of my Instrument & not letting it be ill
> used in any respect. – Do not allow anything to be put
> on it, but what is very light. – I hope you will try to
> make out some other tune besides the Hermit.
>
> (*Letters*, p. 428)

One suspects that little Caroline, having mastered,
probably after some struggle, Giordani's once-popular
air, *The Hermit*, tended to play it *ad nauseam*, or at least
more frequently than her aunts cared to listen to it.
Hence Jane Austen's suggestion that some enlargement of
her niece's repertoire would not come amiss.

Caroline's visit to Chawton was not forgotten when,
in January, 1817, a few months before her death, Aunt
Jane wrote her a letter which concluded with this charming
postscript:

> The Piano Forté often talks of you; – in various keys,
> tunes & expressions I allow – but be it Lesson or
> Country Dance, Sonata or Waltz, *you* are really it's
> constant Theme.
>
> (*Letters*, p. 473)

and a later letter to Caroline, written on March 14th, ends
thus:

> The Piano Forte's Duty, & will be happy to see you
> whenever you can come.
>
> (*Letters*, p. 512)

Despite the onset of her fatal disease and her growing
weakness at this time, Jane Austen continued to send
encouragement and advice to her niece about her piano-
forte-playing. Caroline, it appears, had no pianoforte of
her own at Steventon Parsonage, and relied on the use of
instruments belonging to accommodating neighbours.
Jane Austen expressed delight about a grand pianoforte
lately arrived at Steventon Manor (a house owned by her
brother Edward, and rented to a Mr Digweed), and that

Caroline was to have the use of the instrument:

> You send me Great News indeed my dear Caroline about Mr Digweed . . . & a Grand Piano Forte. I wish it had been a small one, as then you might have pretended Mr D's rooms were too damp to be fit for it, & offered to take charge of it at the Parsonage.
>
> (*Letters*, pp. 473–4)

and on March 26th, when her illness was already well advanced, Aunt Jane was still pursuing the subject:

> I wish you could practise your fingering oftener. – Would it not be a good plan for you to go & live entirely at Mr Wm. Digweed's? – He could not desire any other remuneration than the pleasure of hearing you practise.
>
> (*Letters*, p. 490)

But the delicately humorous tone of these letters to her twelve-year-old niece conceals the sad fact that Jane Austen's failing health had already forced her to give up her own playing. We know that towards the end of February she had tried over some dance music sent her by another niece, that very Fanny who had been with her in London and shared her admiration for Mr Haden ('much obliged for the Quadrilles which I am grown to think pretty enough, though of course they are inferior to the Cotillions of my own day'), but by mid-March, when she finally ceased literary composition, Jane Austen, for all her outward self-control and her brave attempts at optimism, must have realised the seriousness of her condition. Her recognition of the fact that she no longer had the strength for her customary morning practice hour was soon followed by her final abandonment of her uncompleted novel, *Sanditon*. Thus the moment when Jane Austen closed her instrument for the last time becomes, for all who love her work, a tragic symbol for the premature silencing of her all-too-short literary career.

CHAPTER IV

The Minor Works and Northanger Abbey

IN *Sense and Sensibility*, the first of Jane Austen's novels to be published, we meet one of her most musical heroines. Marianne Dashwood plays the pianoforte and sings, certainly with great feeling, and probably with technical fluency as well in view of the long hours she devotes to practising. But her enthusiasm and application are evidently their own reward, for she rarely has the good luck to perform for an appreciative audience. Even Elinor, her beloved sister, is not above holding a private conversation with another young woman, safe in the knowledge that they cannot be overhead while Marianne is giving them 'the powerful protection of a very magnificent concerto'.

Sense and Sensibility, as we know it, was, of course, preceded by a great deal of experimental writing. There is a school of Jane Austen scholarship which is at pains to prove that her juvenilia, as well as her unfinished novel known as *The Watsons* and the short but vivid epistolary novel, *Lady Susan*, were all used by her as quarries for her later and greater works. With these theories Professor Robert Liddell does not wholly agree: he says, quite simply, that it is not the way novelists work, and, as an experienced novelist himself, he is likely to know more about such matters than many other Jane Austen scholars.[15] Nevertheless, there may be a hint of what was to become one of the most important themes (that implicit in its title) of *Sense and Sensibility* in an unfinished

31

attempt at a novel in epistolary form, called *Lesley Castle*,
at which Jane Austen worked in 1792, her seventeenth year.

The three volumes of her juvenilia consist mainly of
short, and usually very sharp *jeux d'esprit* in which the
writer's prime object was to divert herself and her family
with comic exaggerations of the more absurd aspects of
the popular literature of the time. They contain few
references to music. Only in *Lesley Castle*, already mentioned, and in *Catharine, or the Bower*, written in the same
year, are there passages which touch, in the one case on
the part played by music in developing 'sensibility', and
in the other on the, to modern minds, curious emphasis
given to music in Jane Austen's time as a valuable 'acquirement' for girls who are 'on the catch' for husbands.

In *Lesley Castle*, Charlotte Lutterell, a thoroughly
domesticated, down-to-earth girl, whose main passion
in life is cooking, contrasts her own character and
interests with those of her sister, Eloisa:

> Never to be sure were there two more different Dis-
> positions in the World. We both loved Reading. *She*
> preferred Histories, & *I* Receipts. She loved drawing
> Pictures, and I drawing Pullets. No one could sing a
> better Song than She, and no one make a better Pye
> than I. – And so it has always continued since we have
> been no longer Children. The only difference is that all
> disputes on the superior excellence of our Employments
> *then* so frequent are now no more. We have for many
> years entered into an agreement always to admire each
> other's works; I never fail listening to *her* music, & she
> is as constant in eating *my* pies.
>
> (*Minor Works*, p. 129)

But Eloisa, frustrated in love, allows her side of the
arrangement to lapse:

> The Agreement we had entered into of admiring each
> other's productions she no longer seemed to regard . . .
> however . . . having formed my plan . . . I was deter-
> mined to let her have her own way & not even to make
> her a single reproach. My Scheme was . . . not to say so

much as 'Thank you Eloisa'; tho' I had for many years constantly hollowed whenever she played, *Bravo, Bravissimo, Encora, Da Capo, allegretto, con espressione,* and *Poco presto* with many other such outlandish words, all of them as Eloisa told me expressive of my Admiration; and so indeed I suppose they are, as I see some of them in every Page of every Music book, being the Sentiments I imagine of the Composer. I executed my Plan with great Punctuality; I can not say success, for Alas! my silence while she played seemed not in the least to displease her; on the contrary she actually said to me one day 'Well Charlotte, I am very glad to find that you have at last left off that ridiculous custom of applauding my Execution on the Harpsichord.'

(Minor Works, pp. 129–130)

All this, of course, is in a vein of pure burlesque, and perhaps it may seem a little far-fetched to suggest a possible derivation of Elinor and Marianne from the practical, one-track-minded Charlotte and the 'artistic' Eloisa. Yet the idea of two sister heroines of contrasting temperaments, one of them musical, which was to be fully worked out in *Sense and Sensibility* and used again (though with much less thematic importance) in *Pride and Prejudice,* is certainly present in *Lesley Castle,* even though Charlotte and Eloisa are no more than roughly-drawn figures of fun and farce.

In this early skit there are two other points of some interest: Charlotte's absurd use of Italian words, mostly musical terms, which she does not really understand, indicates that the seventeen-year-old authoress understood them very well; and it also seems to contain the seed of Jane Austen's distaste for the use of 'smart' foreign words in spoken English; a distaste which was to find its ultimate expression in the appalling Mrs Elton, with her *caro sposo,* as well as in her prototype, Mrs Robert Watson, who affectedly wishes to be 'treated quite *en famille*' by her own relations; and then there is the reference to a harpsichord rather than to a pianoforte, of which there will be more to say later.

Catharine, an early and not very successful attempt in the narrative style, which did not get very far, also contains some references to music, among them the only mention of an opera in the whole of Jane Austen's writings (her letters excepted). The heroine, Catharine Percival, who leads a very circumscribed life in the country, looks forward to the arrival of visitors:

> The day of their arrival so long expected, at length came, and the Noise of the Coach & 4 as it drove round the sweep, was to Catharine a more interesting sound than the Music of an Italian Opera, which to most Heroines is the hight of Enjoyment.
>
> (*Minor Works*, p. 197)

This is in the same matter-of-fact tone as the opening chapter of *Northanger Abbey*, where we are given a description of an even more unheroic heroine, Catherine Moreland.

Catharine Percival is anticipating with particular pleasure the companionship of one of the new arrivals, Miss Stanley, a girl of about her own age. But Camilla Stanley disappoints her:

> She was not inelegant in her appearance . . . but those Years which ought to have been spent in the attainment of useful knowledge and Mental Improvement, had all been bestowed in learning Drawing, Italian and Music, more especially the latter.
>
> (*Minor Works*, p. 198)

It is evident that, even at the age of seventeen, Jane Austen was already critical of the kind of education which gave pride of place to fashionable acquirements at the expense of solid reading. Miss Stanley proves to be utterly ignorant of such subjects as history and politics:

> [Catharine] received no information from her but in fashions, and no Amusement but in her performance on the Harpsichord.
>
> (*Minor Works*, p. 201)

But it turns out that, despite Catharine's superior mental

development, her own artistic 'acquirements' have not been neglected: Camilla's brother, Edward Stanley, arrives unexpectedly, and very soon he begins to flatter Catharine by pointed attentions:

> He was delighted with her Drawings, and enchanted with her performance on the Harpsichord.
>
> (*Minor Works*, p. 229)

Here again, Jane Austen clings to the word harpsichord, from which we may logically deduce that in 1792 the Austens themselves had not yet acquired one of the more modern pianofortes. This is a little surprising; for though Broadwood's, by now the leaders of their trade in Britain, were still making a few harpsichords in the early 1790s, their sales of pianofortes, begun in 1773, had so greatly expanded that the day of the harpsichord as the universal family instrument in England was virtually over. Evidently the Austens were musically behind the times.

The date of the composition of Jane Austen's short epistolary novel, *Lady Susan*, is still the subject of speculation. The existing manuscript is not the original draft but a fair copy, two sheets of which are watermarked 1805, but it is evidently a work of an earlier date. Authorities differ as to how much earlier: Dr Chapman thought that it was written about 1803;[16] Mr Southam, on the other hand, suggests that it is a still earlier work, perhaps as early as 1793-4,[17] and if this is so, then Jane Austen must have become aware that the harpsichord was already an old-fashioned instrument very shortly after she wrote *Catharine* and *Lesley Castle*, for in *Lady Susan* we find her first mention of a pianoforte.

It is from Lady Susan herself, beautiful and fascinating but the epitome of worldliness and cold-hearted materialism, that we have the clearest exposition of the importance given in fashionable circles to the musical attainments of young girls about to be thrown on the marriage market. The still youthful authoress's astonishingly ruthless revelation of Lady Susan's evil and shallow mentality allows her to express her own disgust at a society which could tolerate such a state of affairs. Here is Lady Susan writing to her particular friend, Mrs Johnson, a woman of her own ilk, about her plans for her unloved daughter, Frederica:

> I want her to play & sing with some portion of Taste, & a good deal of assurance, as she has *my* hand and arm, & a tolerable voice. *I* was so much indulged in my infant years that I was never obliged to attend to anything, & consequently am without those accomplishments which are now necessary to finish a pretty Woman. Not that I am an advocate for the prevailing fashion of acquiring a perfect knowledge in all the Languages Arts and Sciences; it is throwing time away; to be Mistress of French, Italian, German, Music, Singing, Drawing &c. will gain a Woman some applause, but will not add one Lover to her list. Grace and Manner after all are of the greatest importance. I do not mean therefore that Frederica's acquirements should be more than super-ficial. (*Minor Works*, p. 253)

Lady Susan, it will be seen, makes a distinction between 'music' and singing.

Later in the story Frederica runs away from the school in London where her mother has placed her, and eventually arrives at Churchill, the estate of Lady Susan's relations by marriage, the Vernons, where her Ladyship is a self-invited guest. Lady Susan is at pains to prevent Frederica from having tête-à-tête conversations with Mrs Vernon, and does so by incarcerating the unfortunate girl in her dressing-room for hours on end, ostensibly so that she may practise the pianoforte without disturbing anyone. Mrs Vernon, writing to her mother, Lady de Courcy, mentions that,

> the small Pianoforté has been removed within these few days at Lady Susan's request, into her Dressing room, & Frederica spends great part of the day there; *prac-tising* it is called, but I seldom hear any noise when I pass that way. (*Minor Works*, p. 271)

In Jane Austen's letters and in her few extant manuscripts 'pianoforte' is usually written as two words, both beginning with a capital, and often with the final 'e' decorated by an acute accent. Apart from the accent, which seems to have been an orthological peculiarity of her own, this way of writing 'pianoforte' was common practice at the time (*Plate* XII), but Jane Austen is not consistent about it. Sometimes she writes one word or the other, sometimes both, without capitals; sometimes she omits the accent, and occasionally she reduces Piano to a mere 'P'.[18]

The fragment of a novel known as *The Watsons* contains no reference to music or musicians beyond the sound of 'the first scrape of a violin', heard as some of the principal characters arrive at the assembly room of an inn for a ball. Mr Southam has drawn attention to the fact that Jane Austen originally wrote of a violin being tuned, but later replaced 'tuning' with the much more colloquial 'scrape'.[19] It is possible to doubt whether this is a change for the better, for the word 'tuning' conveys something of the excited anticipation of pleasure which immediately precedes the opening of a ball, whereas 'scrape' not only lacks any such evocative overtones but also leaves one with the idea that the dance music will probably be played in a dishearteningly rough-and-ready manner.

There might have been a good deal more about music in Jane Austen's last, uncompleted novel, known now as *Sanditon*, though here it is the harp, and not the pianoforte, which is mentioned more than once. Jane Austen had plenty of opportunity to see and hear harp-playing in her later years, for there was at least one harpist among her near relations – her niece, Fanny Knight. In *Sanditon*, the arrival of the Parker family with their guest, Charlotte Heywood, at the small seaside resort is greeted by the sound of a harp, heard through the upper casement window of a baker's shop – a sound to gladden the ears of Mr Parker, whose business speculations are bound up with the development of Sanditon as a watering place. It signifies the arrival of summer visitors (no member of a baker's family, it is implied, would aspire to the playing of so essentially 'elegant' an instrument as the harp).

Another summer visitor, the elder of two Miss Beauforts, is also equipped with a harp:

> The Miss Bs – though naturally preferring any thing to Smallness & Retirement, yet having in the course of the Spring been involved in the inevitable expense of six new Dresses each . . . were constrained to be satisfied with Sanditon also . . . There, with the hire of a Harp for one, & the purchase of some Drawing paper for the other . . . they meant to be very economical, very elegant & very secluded; with the hope on Miss Beaufort's side, of praise & celebrity from all who walked within the sound of her instrument.
>
> (*Minor Works*, p. 421)

The value of the harp as a domestic instrument, and its superiority to the pianoforte for the display of feminine charms (more particularly of feminine arms) had been recognised from quite early in the eighteenth century. Jane Austen, a pianist herself, establishes her earlier musical young ladies at the keyboard, but there are references to harps in all the Austen novels except *Northanger Abbey*. While there are no harpists among the heroines of *Sense and Sensibility*, *Pride and Prejudice* and *Emma*, we hear of an amateur harpist at the musical party attended by the Miss Dashwoods towards the end of their stay in London (*Sense and Sensibility*, p. 250); we learn from Miss Bingley that Georgiana Darcy studies the harp as well as the pianoforte (*Pride and Prejudice*, p. 48), and in *Emma* (p. 301) the instrument is mentioned by Mrs Elton in the course of her vulgar assessment of Jane Fairfax's prospects in the 'governess trade'. It is in *Mansfield Park* that we find for the first time, a lady harpist (Mary Crawford) playing a leading role, and in *Persuasion* one at least of the Miss Musgroves (it is never made quite clear which one) owns and plays a harp. In *Sanditon*, however, harps begin to proliferate and, as we have seen, they could even be hired there by summer visitors, small and undeveloped though the place might be.

Catherine Morland, the heroine of *Northanger Abbey*, plays neither the harp nor the pianoforte. In fact she has no talents at all and is not even particularly beautiful, for she is the very antithesis of the typical heroine of those novels, principally the works of Mrs Radcliffe, which Jane Austen, in *Northanger Abbey*, holds up to ridicule. It is not a question in Catherine's case, as perhaps it was in Fanny Price's, of dormant talents awaiting development. Catherine has tried to learn the pianoforte and has failed:

> Her mother wished her to learn music; and Catherine was sure she should like it, for she was very fond of tinkling the keys of the old forlorn spinnet; so, at eight years old she began. She learnt a year, and could not bear it; – and Mrs Morland, who did not insist on her daughters being accomplished in spite of incapacity or distaste, allowed her to leave off. The day which dismissed the music-master was one of the happiest of Catherine's life.
>
> (*Northanger Abbey*, p. 14)

In time, however, Catherine learns to sit still and listen to music with some attention:

> At fifteen appearances were mending . . . and though there seemed no chance of her throwing a whole party into raptures by a prelude on the pianoforte, of her own composition, she could listen to other people's performance with very little fatigue.
>
> (*Northanger Abbey*, pp. 14, 16)

Catherine goes to Bath with her good friends, Mr and Mrs Allen, and there she attends Rauzzini's Wednesday evening concerts, as we learn from her first conversation with Henry Tilney:

> 'Have you been to the theatre?'
> 'Yes, sir, I was at the play on Tuesday.'
> 'To the concert?'
> 'Yes, sir, on Wednesday.'
>
> (*Northanger Abbey*, p. 26)

Dr Chapman thought that Jane Austen probably used the 1798 calendar for *Northanger Abbey*. The chronology of the novel takes Catherine to Bath at the end of January: so the first concert after her arrival (it was advertised in the *Bath Chronicle*'s issue for January 25th) will have taken place on February 7th. The names of the artists were announced in the newspaper but there was not much information given about the music to be performed. However, we know that Catherine must have heard a violin concerto played by a boy prodigy, Master Taylor, and a 'Piano-Forte' concerto played by a Mrs Miles, and that she listened (perhaps with rather closer attention) to the singing of Miss Comer, Mr Nield, and last, but very far from least, Madame Mara.

Mara (née Gertrud Schmeling) was one of the greatest singers of the eighteenth century and probably the first diva to be born a German. Her career had been full of drama and incident, and though she was nearly fifty in 1798, and well past her prime as a singer, she was still a sensation, and doubtless the talk of Bath during her brief visit there. Her young *cicisbeo*, a singer named Florio, was travelling with her and he also took part in the concert.[20]

Mrs Allen, after a critical appraisal of Madame Mara's gown and celebrated diamonds, doubtless allowed her attention to wander from the music to the sartorial elegance of the fashionable audience, but Catherine, we know, will have been able to listen to the chief of the concert 'with very little fatigue'. Was she favourably impressed by Madame Mara, or did she secretly prefer the 'sweet, plaintive tones of our own little Syren, Miss Comer' (to quote the *Bath Chronicle* of March 1st)? Certainly Catherine will have been too new to the wonders of Bath, and too unsure of her own taste, to hazard an opinion of the singers' relative merits, if pressed to do so by Mr Tilney.

Mara gave a matinée concert for her own benefit on the morning of Satuday, February 17th, but we know that Mrs Allen and Catherine cannot have attended it, for it was on that very morning that their first, fateful meeting with the Thorpe family took place in the Pump Room. It is unlikely, however, that religious scruples kept them away from Rauzzini's concert on February 21st (Ash Wednesday), where they will have heard 'the playful ease and elegance of Signor Vigadoni's style of singing' and 'the substantial tones of Rovedini's majestic voice', as well as various 'religious' choruses by Handel. A writer in a Bath newspaper, complaining about the rather sparse attendace at this concert, assured his readers that it had been 'an elegant and innocent entertainment', and one well suited to the occasion.

As Rauzzini's Wednesday concerts appear to have been discontinued during Lent Catherine probably heard no more public music-making before she left with the Tilneys for Northanger, but we must hope that she derived a great deal more enjoyment than her creator appears to have done from those of the celebrated impresario's generously proportioned and carefully rehearsed concerts which she attended.

CHAPTER V

Sense and Sensibility

NONE OF Jane Austen's early writings, least of all *Love and Friendship*, that exuberant and highly amusing parody of the novel of exaggerated sentimentality of which Mackenzie's *Man of Feeling* and Madame d'Arblay's *Camilla* are prime examples, prepare one in any way for the deeply-felt emotion and the burning, almost physical pain of the heartbreak suffered by poor Marianne in *Sense and Sensibility*, its authoress's first published work.

Marianne Dashwood may have been foolish, opinionated and headstrong, but her agonies after Willoughby abandoned her would melt a heart of stone. Of course she overdid everything: she was too intense about poetry ('those beautiful lines which have frequently almost driven me wild'), about music, about the beauties of nature, and, inevitably, about love; and to some readers her fervent enthusiasms, like her frequent lack of thought for the feelings of others and her bland, teen-age confidence in the absolute rightness of her often absurd opinions, are too irritating to be forgiven. Even her creator strongly disapproved of her behaviour and meted out to her a severe punishment for it. Yet Marianne's yearning for all that life can give and her delight in natural and artistic beauty deserve much more sympathy than they usually receive, for fundamentally she is on the side of the angels. She has no use for the second-rate, the humdrum or the vulgar; she tries to make the most and the best of every passing moment, and she works hard, always striving for a greater development of her considerable artistic gift.

Willoughby was Marianne's first love (and, one suspects, her last, for it is doubtful if she ever felt more than esteem, respect and a sort of calm affection for Colonel Brandon, whom she was eventually to marry), yet she was, in a sense, madly in love long before she met Willoughby: she had fallen in love with art. It is because Willoughby is able to share her passion for the arts in general and for music in particular that their electrically immediate physical attraction for one another quickly develops, at least on Marianne's part, into something much deeper and more lasting.

> His society became gradually her most exquisite enjoyment. They read, they talked, they sang together; his musical talents were considerable.
>
> (*Sense and Sensibility*, p. 48)

Whether she could ever have loved anyone who did not share her cultural enthusiasms is very doubtful, for she was always ready to base her opinion of other people on their attitude to the arts. Even Edward Ferrars, whom she believes (mistakenly) to be secretly engaged to her sister, Elinor, is judged by her and found wanting:

> 'I am afraid, Mamma, he has no real taste. Music seems scarcely to attract him . . .'
>
> (*Sense and Sensibility*, p. 17)

She is naturally and rightly disgusted by the lack of attention and true appreciation given to her own playing and singing by the Middleton family:

> In the evening, as Marianne was discovered to be musical, she was invited to play. The instrument was unlocked, everybody prepared to be charmed, and Marianne, who sang very well, at their request went through the chief of the songs which Lady Middleton had brought into the family on her marriage, and which, perhaps, had lain ever since in the same position on the pianoforté; . . . Marianne's performance was highly applauded. Sir John was loud in his admiration at the end of every song, and as loud in his conversation with

the others while every song lasted. Lady Middleton
frequently called him to order, wondered how anyone's
attention could be diverted from music for a moment,
and asked Marianne to sing a particular song which
Marianne had just finished.

(Sense and Sensibility, p. 35)

It is evident that Marianne's musical proficiency was
quite exceptional, and that it went far beyond the mere
repetition of songs and pianoforte solos which she already
knew well, for on this occasion she performed a very
difficult feat: she read at sight, and simultaneously,
the words, the vocal line and the accompaniment of several
songs, most of which must have been quite new to her. In
a girl of seventeen this evinces an unusually high degree of
musicianship.

Among Marianne's listeners there was one who attended
to her singing with interest and in silence:

Colonel Brandon alone, of all the party, heard her
without being in raptures. He paid her only the compliment of attention; and she felt a respect for him on
the occasion, which the others had reasonably forfeited
by their shameless want of taste. His pleasure in music,
though it amounted not to that extatic delight which
alone could sympathise with her own, was estimable
when contrasted against the horrible insensibility of the
others.

(Sense and Sensibility, p. 35)

The Colonel is quiet and serious by nature. He is the
exact opposite of the fascinating Willoughby, who reminds
one forcibly of those artistic young men, much more
common in Russian than in English literature, who shine
socially by singing, playing, reading romantic poetry and
generally charming polite society, while at the same time
leading private lives of an almost brutal dissipation.

It was during Willoughby's very first call at Barton
Cottage to enquire after Marianne on the morning following her accident that she learned, to her delight, that 'his
musical talents were considerable'. They were evidently

not limited to singing, though his ability to sing duets with her certainly helped the quick promotion of their romantic attachment. Love is a favourite theme of the vocal music of the period (of any period, for that matter), and we may be sure that Willoughby's eyes met Marianne's in many a speaking glance as 'the sweet sound of their united voices' filled the Dashwood's little drawing-room. But it is highly probable that they played pianoforte duets as well (a much more intimate exercise), for Willoughby's ability to copy out music implies a degree of musical training considerably beyond the range of the average amateur singer. The art of music-copying cannot be acquired without considerable practice, and it usually goes with the study of an instrument rather than with a musical knowledge limited to the reading and performance of vocal music. Printed music was expensive and hard to come by in those days, and hand-written collections of songs and piano-forte music were to be found in every household.[21]

Colonel Brandon earned Marianne's respect by his unspoken appreciation of her musical talent, but of course, once Willoughby appeared on the scene she had eyes for no one else; his ardour and charm, to say nothing of his youth and good looks swept her off her feet, leaving the worthy and ever-faithful Colonel waiting in the wings until the drama of Marianne's tragic love affair had run its course and he could at last step forward to pick up the pieces of her broken heart. It is doubtful, however, whether Marianne became heart-whole again. Her period of utter felicity was very short, but it was far too intense ever to be forgotten. After Willoughby abandons her (though at first she believes their separation to be only temporary) she gives herself over completely to the indulgence of her grief and finds in music a natural outlet for it:

> She played over every favourite song that she had been used to play to Willoughby, every air in which their voices had been oftenest joined, and sat at the instrument gazing on every line of music that he had written out for her, till her heart was so heavy that no further

sadness could be gained; and this nourishment of grief
was every day applied. She spent whole hours at the
pianoforté, alternately singing and crying; her voice
often totally suspended by her tears.

(Sense and Sensibility, p. 83)

Her distress is such that she can at first bear to see no
one but her own family – least of all such people as
the Middletons, whom she despises for their philistinism
and their vulgarities of thought and speech. Sir John calls
at Barton Cottage and asks where Marianne is:

'Has she run away because we are come? I see her
instrument is open.'

(Sense and Sensibility, p. 105)

The fact that Marianne's pianoforte is open tells him
that it has very recently been in use. This is an interesting
point, for it reminds us that pianofortes were, in Jane
Austen's time, invariable kept shut when they were not
being played, and sometimes, as in the case of Lady
Middleton's instrument, actually locked. Lady Middleton
probably had good reason to lock her pianoforte, for her
unruly brood of children (who, as even Lucy Steele
admitted, were indulged 'the outside of enough') would
soon have played havoc with the regulation of its keys and
would probably have broken half the strings had they been
able to meddle with it. But there is no doubt that the
wooden-framed pianofortes of the time, being much less
sturdy than they were to become after the invention of the
cast-iron frame, needed constant care and protection.
Instruments were not only kept closed (and sometimes
locked), but they were often covered by a thick cloth.
Jane Austen herself, as we have seen, though glad to allow
her little niece, Caroline, to use her pianoforte, was
understandably anxious that it should not be 'ill used',
and that nothing should be put on it 'but what is very
light'.

After a period of extravagant misery following
Willoughby's departure, Marianne, still believing that

they will be eventually reunited, calms her nerves
sufficiently to go into company, though only for the sake of
her mother and sisters. She will not, however, do more than
sit in silent self-communion while they visit the Middletons
(who appear to be their only neighbours), and she still
seizes every opportunity to indulge herself with her one
consolation – music.

Lady Middleton proposes a rubber of Casino, and
Marianne is quick to avoid being involved in it:

> 'Your Ladyship will have the goodness to excuse *me* –
> you know I detest cards. I shall go to the piano-forte;
> I have not touched it since it was tuned.' And without
> further ceremony, she walked to the instrument.
> *(Sense and Sensibility*, p. 144)

Poor Elinor is frequently called upon to repair the
damage done to the fabric of social conventions by her
sister's scorn of dissimulation and disregard of normal
politeness. On this occasion Elinor does her best, but it is
not very convincing. She tries to cover Marianne's
brusque refusal to play cards by saying,

> 'Marianne can never keep long from that instrument
> you know ma'am . . . and I do not wonder at it; for it
> is the very best toned piano-forté I ever heard.'
> *(Sense and Sensibility*, p. 145)

The rich Middletons' pianoforte probably *was* an excellent one, but everyone knew that Marianne was
accustomed to one at least as good. We are told, early in
the story, that the small amount of furniture removed
from Norland to Barton included 'an handsome pianoforte of Marianne's,' an instrument which would have been
purchased during the Dashwoods former days of wealth
and grandeur and which will have been quite the equal
of, if not superior to the Middletons' pianoforte. It is at this
point in the novel that Elinor has her famous conversation
with Lucy Steele under cover of the 'very magnificent
concerto' with which Marianne gives them such 'powerful
protection'. What, one wonders, was the work Marianne

played? *Sense and Sensibility* was begun in 1797 but was much revised during the twelve years which preceded its first publication in 1811. By that date the most 'magnificent' of all concertos, Beethoven's Fifth Concerto, in E flat, the so-called 'Emperor', was already in existence; but it is far more likely that Jane Austen had in mind one of the 'Grand' concertos by such composers as Dussek, Cramer, or Steibelt which were brought out in vast numbers by London music publishers of the day.

We may as well take our leave of poor Marianne, seated at the pianoforte, 'wrapped in her own music and her own thoughts', while she fills the air with cascades of brilliant passage-work. For though in the third volume of *Sense and Sensibility* we catch a brief glimpse of her playing 'lessons' on the pianoforte in Mrs Jenning's London home, this occurs only towards the end of the Dashwood sisters' London visit and after Marianne has partially recovered from the terrible emotional breakdown she suffered on realising Willoughby's faithlessness to her. It is significant that a musical party which the sisters attended shortly before they left London is seen only through Elinor's eyes:

> The events of the evening were not very remarkable. The party, like other musical parties, comprehended a great many people who had real taste for the performance, and a great many more who had none at all; and the performers themselves were, as usual, in their own estimation, and that of their immediate friends, the first private performers in England.
>
> As Elinor was neither musical, nor affecting to be so, she made no scruple of turning her eyes from the grand pianoforté, whenever it suited her, and unrestrained even by the presence of a harp, and a violoncello, would fix them at pleasure on any other object in the room.
>
> *(Sense and Sensibility, p. 250)*

It will be noticed that Jane Austen does not censure Elinor for her lack of interest in music. Yet the programme appears to have been so pleasantly varied – three instruments are mentioned and doubtless there were vocal items as well – that Elinor, one feels, should have made more effort to listen to it, though the amateurishness of the performances could, perhaps, be regarded as some excuse for her inattention. As for Marianne, who was also at the party, we know that in normal circumstances she would have been an interested and probably a severely critical listener. But the very fact that she is not mentioned at all underlines her total abstraction from events and her numbed responses to what is going on around her.

Jane Austen's first published novel, with all its irony, humour and youthful vitality, is, on the whole, a sad story. Marianne's extreme 'sensibility' is not the *cause* of her misfortune, it only increases its degree, and one is left uncertain whether the authoress herself believed that a refined susceptibility to the effect of music on the emotions was more likely to undermine the nerves, and therefore the strength needed to overcome life's difficulties, than to provide a sensitive soul with a valuable means of consolation and support when weighed down by affliction.

CHAPTER VI

Pride and Prejudice

WHAT WAS perhaps Jane Austen's own view of music – that it was an art which had considerable social value but which ought not to be allowed to absorb too much time or to generate too much 'enthusiasm' – is implied by her use of it as a symbol for Marianne Dashwood's extravagant emotionalism. The authoress seems to be suggesting that so intense a devotion to the art as Marianne's can, at least in the case of an already highly-strung young girl, lead to no good. In her next work, that masterpiece of comedy, *Pride and Prejudice*, the very attractive heroine is not allowed to possess any artistic abilities which exceed the average.

Elizabeth Bennet is a thoroughly natural, healthy girl, and she is also highly intelligent. She is as poised and sensible as Elinor Dashwood (though without a trace of the latter's slight priggishness) but she is in no way outstandingly talented. It is as if Jane Austen preferred that the heroine ('as delightful a creature as ever appeared in print, and how I shall be able to tolerate those who do not like *her* at least I do not know') with whom she is herself often identified, should not outshine her creator in any particular drawing-room accomplishment. It is useful to the plot that Elizabeth should play and sing but it is not necessary that she should do so more than 'well enough'.

A less important character in the novel, one who does have a serious, not to say solemn, attitude to the arts, and who devotes much of her time to the study of books and music, is given highly satirical treatment in *Pride and*

Prejudice, her cultural proclivities being curiously equated with her unfortunate lack of personal beauty:

> . . . in consequence of being the only plain one of the family [Mary] worked hard for knowledge and accomplishments.

(Pride and Prejudice, p. 25)

Poor Mary Bennet! One is supposed to laugh at her for her bluestocking ways, but she is the only one of the Bennet girls whose future should give the reader cause for concern. She is as portionless as her sisters ('one thousand pounds in the four per cents' is all she can look forward to as a support after her father's death), but, as she has very little chance of gaining an 'establishment' through marriage, she is likely to become as needy, as silly and as despised in her old age as Miss Bates. No wonder she did what she could to attract attention. She could not alter her looks: so she tried, by 'improving her mind', to gain a little local celebrity as an intellectual. That she possessed no exceptional talents to match her application was her misfortune. It is often overlooked that there is another minor character in *Pride and Prejudice,* one of whom we hear more than we see, who spends quite as much time at the keyboard as does Mary Bennet. But Georgiana Darcy escapes any of the ridicule and contempt allotted to Mary, presumably because she is handsome and rich, for we have it only on the very 'tainted' authority of Miss Bingley that 'her performance on the piano-forte is exquisite'.

Elizabeth Bennet's ability to sing to her own accompaniment, and do it reasonably well, is put to the test quite early in the story. The Bennets' neighbours, the Lucas family, give a large party to which most of Meryton society is invited, and Charlotte Lucas, Elizabeth's particular friend, presses her to sing:

> 'I am going to open the instrument, Eliza, and you know what follows.'
> 'You are a very strange creature by way of a friend! – always wanting me to play and sing before any body and

every body! – If my vanity had taken a musical turn,
you would have been invaluable, but as it is, I would
really rather not sit down before those who must be in
the habit of hearing the very best performers.'

(*Pride and Prejudice*, p. 24)

It is odd that the Lucas girls themselves, who must surely
have been taught music, since the drawing-room at Lucas
Lodge boasts a pianoforte, do not perform at their own
party, but perhaps it was not their place to shine on such
an occasion. We hear only of Elizabeth's and Mary's performances. Elizabeth, as the elder sister, leads:

> Her performance was pleasing, though by no means
> capital. After a song or two, and before she could reply
> to the entreaties of several that she would sing again,
> she was eagerly succeeded at the instrument by her
> sister Mary . . . Mary had neither genius nor taste;
> and though vanity had given her application, it had
> given her likewise a pedantic air and conceited manner,
> which would have injured a higher degree of excellence
> than she had reached. Elizabeth, easy and unaffected,
> had been listened to with much more pleasure, though
> not playing half so well; and Mary, at the end of a long
> concerto, was glad to purchase praise and gratitude by
> Scotch and Irish airs, at the request of her younger
> sisters.

(*Pride and Prejudice*, p. 25)

Elizabeth has the merit of being very well aware of her
own limitations, and evidently she knows when to stop.
It was foolish of Mary to launch into a concerto, of all
things, on such an occasion, but note Jane Austen's qualify-
ing adjective: it was a *long* concerto. With one well-chosen
word we are made aware of the half-stifled yawns, the
mobile eyebrows and the rising hum of conversation which
accompany Mary as she plays doggedly on through
exposition, development, recapitulation, cadenza and
coda (it may be assumed that she inflicted no more than
the concerto's first movement on her audience). In *Sense
and Sensibility*, Marianne also played a concerto and

nobody listened to it. It was probably quite as long as
Mary's concerto (it could even have been the same work)
but, played by Marianne, it sounded 'magnificent'. Thus
we know that the lack of attention given to it by Lady
Middleton and her guests is a reflection on them and not on
the talent of the performer.

There is, however, a small difficulty about the passage
quoted above: it is stated that Elizabeth's performance
was pleasing, whereas Mary had neither genius (a large
word indeed) or that mysterious attribute, 'taste', of
which more will be said elsewhere. Yet it is admitted that,
of the two, Elizabeth does not play half so well. I have an
idea that it was mostly Mary's unfortunate manner
which counted against her; that she really acquitted herself with considerable competence, and that her lack of
success had more to do with the unsuitable music she
played (unsuited, that is, to the occasion) than with her
playing of it. At least her readiness to play dance music
immediately after the concerto was obliging enough, and
it showed that she was not above climbing off her cultural
pedestal and descending abruptly into the market place.

Elizabeth is next asked to sing while she is staying at
Netherfield Park, the home of Charles Bingley, where
Jane, Elizabeth's elder sister, is the guest of Charles's
sister, Caroline. Jane has caught a chill and Elizabeth has
come to nurse her. Elizabeth leaves her patient for a while
and joins the rest of the party in the drawing-room, where
Mr Darcy is just managing to complete a letter to his
sister, Georgiana, in spite of irritating interruptions from
Caroline Bingley, who clearly has matrimonial designs on
him. Probably as an escape from her unwelcome attentions,
he asks for 'the indulgence of some music'. It is a general
application to the ladies of the party, but at once

> Miss Bingley moved with alacrity to the piano-forte,
> and after a polite request that Elizabeth would lead the
> way, which the other as politely and more earnestly
> negatived, she seated herself.
>
> (*Pride and Prejudice*, p. 51)

Caroline Bingley sings duets with her sister, Mrs Hurst, (Italian airs, we are told) while Elizabeth stands by the instrument, turning over some music lying on it. As she does so she notices how frequently Mr Darcy's eyes are fixed upon her. It is a sign that he is beginning to find her unusually attractive. Miss Bingley, sensing danger, 'varies the charm by a lively Scottish air'. This was the period when 'Scotch Songs' were the rage of polite society, not merely in England but throughout all Europe. The collections brought out by several Edinburgh publishers, often with accompaniments by the greatest composers of the day, among them Haydn, Pleyel and later Beethoven, had an immense sale. The demand soon exceeded the supply, and the composition of fake Scottish melodies became a lucrative trade for impecunious British composers. However, the music Miss Bingley played might not have been one of these pseudo-Scottish songs but a piece of genuine Scottish dance music, since it prompted Mr Darcy to ask Elizabeth if it did not make her wish to 'seize the opportunity of dancing a reel'. It was an oddly uncharacteristic remark for him to make, and, as Elizabeth had already heard his opinion of dancing as an entertainment ('every savage can dance'), it verged on the impolite. Not surprisingly, she 'smiled and made no answer', which obliged him to repeat the question and probably made him wish he had never asked it. Elizabeth, who often seems to possess a maturity well beyond her twenty years, knows very well that silence can be a more effective rebuke than words.

When Jane and Elizabeth returned home 'they found Mary, as usual, deep in the study of thorough bass and human nature'. It is puzzling to find Jane Austen (for it is the authoress herself who speaks here) sneering at a plain girl for studying a branch of musical theory. Why was Mary to be ridiculed for doing something so very well worth while? Had Mr Chard, perhaps, once tried to teach Jane Austen something of thorough bass and failed to arouse her interest? One wonders, too, with whom Mary can have pursued her musical studies, for we know that she

never had the advantage of a London master. She probably had pianoforte lessons from a music teacher living in
Meryton, but she may well have had to struggle with the
science of thorough bass entirely unaided. Surely she
deserved praise rather than mockery for her efforts?

Mary receives another 'set-down' a little later on in the
story, when, at the Netherfield Park ball, she is all too
eager to sing to the very large party assembled there:

> Mary's powers were by no means fitted for such a dis
> play; her voice was weak, and her manner affected. –
> Elizabeth was in agonies.
>
> (*Pride and Prejudice*, p. 100)

Elizabeth gives her father a speaking glance to entreat
his interference 'lest Mary should be singing all night'.
He takes the hint and delivers his celebrated snub:

> 'That will do extremely well, child. You have delighted
> us long enough. Let the other young ladies have time to
> exhibit.'
>
> Mary, though pretending not to hear, was somewhat
> disconcerted.
>
> (*Pride and Prejudice*, p. 101)

As well she might be. Mr Bennet's sardonic words must
have seriously injured her ego, as was doubtless his
intention. Elizabeth was sorry for Mary, and regretted her
interference, but it must be admitted that it was a splendidly deflating utterance and one would not have it unsaid for the world. How often, when bored to tears
by the efforts of some self-satisfied musician (nowadays
it is contemporary composers, rather than performers,
who are usually the culprits), one longs to quote, in
ringing tones, Mr Bennet's immortal phrases.

In the second volume of *Pride and Prejudice*, Elizabeth's
playing gives rise to some of the finest scenes of comedy in
all Jane Austen's work – those which describe the heroine's
encounters with Lady Catherine de Bourgh at Rosings.
The subject is first used to contrast Elizabeth's quiet
good manners with Lady Catherine's gross conceit and

inquisitiveness. Although Lady Catherine is already well informed about the Bennet family she wants to know more:

> 'Do you play and sing, Miss Bennet?'
> 'A little.'
> 'Oh! then – some time or other we shall be happy to hear you. Our instrument is a capital one, probably superior to – You shall try it some day. – Do your sisters play and sing?'
> 'One of them does.'
> 'Why did not you all learn? – You ought all to have learned. The Miss Webbs all play, and their father has not so good an income as your's. – Do you draw?'
>
> *(Pride and Prejudice*, p. 164)

Lady Catherine speaks here in the first person plural. It is just possible that 'we' only means herself and her daughter, Anne, but it is infinitely more likely that her vast sense of her own grandeur has accustomed her to use the royal pronoun. Her patronising remarks about 'our instrument' and the crude revelation of her knowledge (doubtless obtained from Mr Collins) of the exact amount of Mr Bennet's income are further symptoms of her insensitivity and overweening self-importance. Lady Catherine continues her impertinent enquiries and Elizabeth bears with her for some time, but when asked point-blank to state her age she amuses herself by refusing to reveal it. Her Ladyship is astounded. She is quite unused to being, as she would put it, 'trifled with'.

The next time we see Elizabeth at Rosings, Lady Catherine's circle has received two important additions: her nephews, Mr Darcy and Colonel Fitzwilliam, have arrived for their annual visit.

Colonel Fitzwilliam is much taken with Elizabeth and seats himself beside her. They are talking animatedly together and discussing music when Lady Catherine interrupts them:

> 'What is that you are saying, Fitzwilliam? What is it you are talking of? What are you telling Miss Bennet?

Let me hear what it is.'

'We are speaking of music, Madam,' said he, when
no longer able to avoid a reply.

'Of music! Then pray speak aloud. It is of all subjects
my delight. I must have my share in the conversation,
if you are speaking of music. There are few people in
England, I suppose, who have more true enjoyment of
music than myself, or a better natural taste. If I had
ever learnt, I should have been a great proficient. And
so would Anne, if her health had allowed her to apply.
I am confident that she would have performed delightfully.'

(*Pride and Prejudice*, p. 173)

This speech of Lady Catherine's is altogether very
strange. Her claim to delight in music and to possess
superior musical taste (that word again!) is followed by the
incredible statement that she has never learnt to play
herself. We have already heard her express sharp disapproval of the fact that of the five Bennet sisters only
two play and sing. How then is it possible that the great
Lady Catherine, the daughter of an earl, rich and pam-
pered from childhood, did not have the benefit of the best
available London master – the great Johann Christian
Bach himself, perhaps? The only clue that suggests itself
is that we have already met, in Jane Austen's Minor
Works, another noble lady, Lady Susan (as unpleasant a
woman as Lady Catherine, though in quite a different
way), who was equally devoid of artistic accomplishments. Lady Susan offered her own explanation for this
lack – that she was so much indulged in her infant years
that she was never obliged to attend to anything – and for
want of something better this must do for Lady Catherine
as well, but it is not a satisfactory solution of the mystery.

Lady Catherine, like many boastful people, can be very
stupid: by speaking of her daughter's similar inability to
play or sing she is led on to refer to Miss de Bourgh's
feeble health. As she is anxious for Darcy to marry his
cousin it is, to say the least, very unwise of her to draw

attention to the poor girl's sickly constitution. However, her doting affection for her puny and colourless offspring is, perhaps, Lady Catherine's one redeeming feature, and in its way it is rather touching.

Lady Catherine's insufferably dictatorial tone and her constant habit of hortation are evident even when she converses with her nephew. Her absurd praise of her daughter's non-existent musical talent reminds her that her niece, Georgiana, really does play the pianoforte:

> 'How does Georgiana get on, Darcy?'
>
> Mr Darcy spoke with affectionate praise of his sister's proficiency.
>
> 'I am very glad to hear such a good account of her,' said Lady Catherine; 'and pray tell her from me, that she cannot expect to excel if she does not practise a great deal.'
>
> 'I assure you, madam,' he replied, 'that she does not need such advice. She practises very constantly.'
>
> 'So much the better. It cannot be done too much; and when I next write to her, I shall charge her not to neglect it on any account. I often tell young ladies that no excellence in music is to be acquired without constant practice. I have told Miss Bennet several times that she will never play really well unless she practises more; and though Mrs Collins has no instrument, she is very welcome, as I have often told her, to come to Rosings every day, and play on the piano forte in Mrs Jenkinson's room. She would be in nobody's way, you know, in that part of the house.'
>
> Mr Darcy looked a little ashamed of his aunt's ill-breeding, and made no answer.
>
> (*Pride and Prejudice*, p. 173)

Mr Darcy's shame needs, perhaps, some explanation today. Mrs Jenkinson's room was evidently the domain of the governess, though the lady herself, having long since ceased 'governing', had dropped further in status to something resembling a superior abigail (was Miss de Bourgh actually mentally, as well as physically feeble, and therefore in need of constant attendance?). As is well

known, governesses in Jane Austen's time were practically
social outcasts whose apartments would be suitably
removed from those of their employers: so 'that part of
the house' implied a proximity to the servants' quarters
which it would have been unsuitable for Elizabeth, as a
'gentleman's daughter', to frequent. Hence Mr Darcy's
awkward feelings. The instrument in Mrs Jenkinson's
room was probably a small square pianoforte, put there
to be out of the way; for it is unlikely that the ex-
governess, if she played at all, was allowed time to indulge
herself with private music-making.

When Elizabeth finally tries Lady Catherine's 'superior'
pianoforte she does so at Colonel Fitzwilliam's request
and not its owner's:

> Colonel Fitzwilliam reminded Elizabeth of having
> promised to play to him; and she sat down directly to
> the instrument. He drew a chair near her. Lady
> Catherine listened to half a song, and then talked, as
> before, to her other nephew; till the latter walked
> away from her and, moving with his usual deliberation
> towards the piano forte, stationed himself so as to
> command a full view of the performer's countenance.
>
> (*Pride and Prejudice*, pp. 173–4)

There follows a scene of brilliant comedy which is full
of subtle meanings and is extraordinarily theatrical in its
effect. Elizabeth, elegant, witty and charming, holds the
centre of the stage. Seated at the pianoforte, she sings for
Colonel Fitzwilliam and then, at a first convenient pause
in the music, turns with an arch smile to Mr Darcy:

> 'You mean to frighten me, Mr Darcy, by coming in all
> this state to hear me? But I will not be alarmed though
> your sister *does* play so well. There is a stubbornness
> about me that can never bear to be frightened at the
> will of others. My courage always rises with every
> attempt to intimidate me.'
>
> (*Pride and Prejudice*, p. 174)

She is, of course, joking; she has not yet consciously admitted to herself what is obvious to the reader – that Mr

Darcy admires her extremely, and that with such a man
admiration is likely to be a much more serious and lasting
matter than with his attractive, but superficial cousin,
who intends no more than a pleasant flirtation – but
feminine instinct prompts her to play one man off against
the other. Darcy's reply –

> 'I shall not say you are mistaken . . . because you
> could not really believe me to entertain any design of
> alarming you; and I have had the pleasure of your ac-
> quaintance long enough to know that you find great
> enjoyment in occasionally professing opinions which, in
> fact, are not your own.'

– causes her much amusement, and we have the strange
feeling that her laughter charms and fascinates not only
her two admirers but a packed auditorium of delighted
onlookers as well.

Elizabeth then turns to Colonel Fitzwilliam and gives
him a witty account of the aloof and unsociable behaviour
which had aroused such resentment against Darcy in
Meryton society during the previous winter. She is paying
off an old score, for he had, within her hearing, refused
the suggestion of his friend, Bingley, that he should dance
with her. Darcy seems to be uncomfortably aware of what
she has in mind, for he says:

> 'Perhaps . . . I should have judged better had I sought
> an introduction, but I am ill qualified to recommend
> myself to strangers . . . I certainly have not the talent
> which some people possess of conversing easily with
> those I have never seen before.'
>
> *(Pride and Prejudice*, p. 175)

Elizabeth, with a better knowledge of her failings than
Darcy of his, uses her limited command of pianoforte
technique to illustrate the point of her reply:

> 'My fingers . . . do not move over this instrument in the
> masterly manner which I see so many women's do.
> They have not the same force or rapidity, and do not
> produce the same expression. But then I have always

supposed it to be my own fault – because I would not take the trouble of practising. It is not that I do not believe *my* fingers as capable as any other women's of superior execution.'

Darcy is too much under the charm of Elizabeth's delightful personality to be offended by her only slightly oblique criticism of his behaviour, but his reply, starting as a compliment, ends lamely:

'You are perfectly right. You have employed your time much better. No one admitted to the privilege of hearing you can think anything wanting. We neither of us perform to strangers.'

(*Pride and Prejudice*, p. 176)

Does he regard it as a 'performance' to be merely polite to people who happen to be outside the immediate circle of his family and friends? And can he not guess that Elizabeth, 'easy and unaffected' as she is, would probably sing and play to strangers with very good grace if politely asked to do so?

Throughout this scene, with its musical allusions and its emotional undercurrents, Lady Catherine has remained in the background (though still visible to our imaginary audience and doubtless busy pontificating to the sycophantic Collinses).

Whether Elizabeth's dialogue with Darcy might have developed even more interestingly we cannot know, because Lady Catherine, suddenly becoming aware that for some time music has been replaced by conversation, demands, as before, to know what they are talking about. Elizabeth immediately begins to play again. Fatuous as ever, Lady Catherine now sets herself up as a music critic. She is well qualified for the position, being unable to perform herself:

Lady Catherine approached, and, after listening for a few minutes, said to Darcy,

'Miss Bennet would not play at all amiss, if she practised more, and could have the advantage of a London

master. She has a very good notion of fingering,
though her taste is not equal to Anne's. Anne would
have been a delightful performer, had her health allowed
her to learn.'

It is lucky that Lady Catherine can invoke 'taste' in her
daughter's praise, since this elusive quality, unlike fingering, is difficult to define and open to a wide range of inter-
pretations.

Lady Catherine continued her remarks on Elizabeth's
performance, mixing with them many instructions on
execution and taste. Elizabeth received them with all
the forbearance of civility; and at the request of the
gentlemen remained at the instrument till her Ladyship's carriage was ready to take them all home.

The histrionic elements in this scene, and, indeed, in
many other scenes in *Pride and Prejudice*, have resulted in
the book's frequent adaptation for stage performance. It
has also been seen in the cinema, on the television screen
and even in the form of a 'musical'. But the impious and
predatory fingers which periodically tamper with Jane
Austen's masterly work sometimes end by burning themselves through the box-office window, for as a whole it
does not lend itself to dramatic presentation quite as
readily as many have supposed.

The one theatrical form for which it has not, so far,
been used is opera. Yet it would be possible to imagine at
least some of its scenes, and certainly the 'quartet' in Lady
Catherine's drawing-room, as part of some ideal but impossible operatic comedy, with a libretto by, perhaps,
Hofmannsthal, and music, of course, by Mozart.
Elizabeth's silvery soprano (tending very slightly towards
the type of voice one associates with soubrette roles – a
Susanna rather than a Pamina), Colonel Fitzwilliam's
elegant and agile tenor and Darcy's firm, noble baritone
would be joined by Lady Catherine's deep, almost masculine contralto tones (as Lady Catherine is as much a
pantomine dame as a *grande dame* her part could even be

given to a male singer *en travestie*). An operatic version of *Pride and Prejudice* is unlikely to be written, however, and we may be thankful for it. No contemporary musical idiom could do justice to the smiling charm, the high spirits and the innate sweetness of Elizabeth Bennet, and no operatic soprano known to me would make a convincing English rose of less than one-and-twenty. In any case, Jane Austen would have strongly opposed any such adaptation of her work. She disliked singing.

CHAPTER VII

Mansfield Park

THE MYTH that Jane Austen, after writing three brilliant novels before she was twenty-five, remained silent for the next seven years and then, on moving to Chawton, set to work and produced three more masterpieces, has long been exploded. The so-called 'Steventon' novels, according to her brother, Henry, were 'the gradual performance of her previous life' (previous, that is, to the time of their publication), and this implies that they were subjected to a long period of ruthless self-criticism and much re-writing. When *Sense and Sensibility* was printed, in 1811, Jane Austen was already living in Chawton and her fourth novel, *Mansfield Park*, was well advanced.

However, though it may not be admissible to speak of the 'Steventon' novels, it is perfectly appropriate to group together *Mansfield Park*, *Emma* and *Persuasion* as the Chawton novels. They were, after all, begun and finished there.

The earlier books, as we have seen, had all made use of music, though in different ways and to different degrees. In *Northanger Abbey* it was used negatively, as an aspect of Catherine Morland's lack of 'heroic' qualifications; in *Sense and Sensibility* it reflected Marianne's emotional excesses, her pianoforte being her only real confidante during much of her disastrous affair with Willoughby; in *Pride and Prejudice* the authoress appeared to approve of music as an agreeable, if superficial diversion but took a curiously philistine view of it as a subject for serious study.

In the three Chawton novels, music is used, on the whole, in a more sympathetic manner than in Jane Austen's earlier books, but it would be a mistake for any enthusiastic 'Janeite', who also happened to be a music-lover, to hope that the novelist herself had, with the passage of time, become a more appreciative listener. Her letters tell us that at the very moment when she was seeing *Emma* (the most 'musical' of her books) through the press she was still deaf to the charms of the singing voice and quite prepared to do battle with 'angelic' Mr Haden over his Shakespearean condemnation of unmusical people as creatures 'fit for every sort of wickedness'. Nevertheless, the Chawton novels all use music in new and interesting ways, both in the structure of their plots and in the revelation of character. In *Mansfield Park*, for instance, though the art is treated with more respect than it was accorded in *Pride and Prejudice*, it is only associated with the 'bad' characters of the story – with the anti-heroine, Mary Crawford, and with the spoiled and selfish Bertram sisters. Mary Crawford, indeed, uses music as a lure to fascinate Edmund Bertram, while poor Fanny Price, unable to compete, looks on in helpless frustration.

Fanny is thought to have been preferred by her creator to any of the other heroines. 'My Fanny', Jane Austen called her, though she never wrote of 'my Emma', 'my Anne', or 'my Elizabeth'. That she allowed Fanny no artistic accomplishments is easily explained: it was to be a very long time before Fanny could be at Mansfield without suffering from her female cousins' derision of her ignorance, from the bullying of her Aunt Norris and from her own overpowering sense of obligation and inferiority. No wonder she shrank from the mere suggestion that she might learn to play the pianoforte or to draw. The simple instinct of self-preservation would have warned her to keep as quiet as possible and to avoid any situation which might place her directly in competition with either Maria or Julia.

Not that it is likely that either of the Miss Bertrams

played or sang really well. As long as their father remained in parliament, and the house in town was kept up, they would, of course, have enjoyed the benefit of the best available London masters. But the 'brilliant accomplishments' with which they were credited in the Mansfield neighbourhood may be taken with a pinch of salt, for we only hear that they sometimes played pianoforte duets, coached, presumably, by their governess, Miss Lee, whose own musical abilities do not appear to have been greatly valued at Mansfield, since they failed to qualify her as a regular member of the drawing-room party. Miss Lee seems never to have mixed with her employers on equal terms, though, until Fanny was old enough to take her place, she was sometimes useful to Lady Bertram as a companion on occasions when the rest of the family was absent.

Poor Fanny, still bewildered, homesick and frightened after her arrival at Mansfield, was too guileless to hide from Maria and Julia that she was 'little struck with the duet they were so good as to play her'; which naturally confirmed the low opinion they had already formed of her on discovering that she possessed 'but two sashes and had never learned French', though I am inclined to think that it showed instinctive musical good taste as well as naive, twelve-year-old sincerity. It was probably Miss Lee who, prompted by Sir Thomas, asked Fanny whether she would like to learn music, for neither her aunts nor her cousins can be imagined as having initiated such an enquiry. The Miss Bertrams would not have cared one way or the other. They were far too interested in, and satisfied with, themselves and, as they grew older, they would have come to regard such musical abilities as they possessed as mere adjuncts to their unassailable position as the reigning belles of Northamptonshire society. Their attitude to Mary Crawford is revealing in this connection: the fact that she was quite an accomplished musician and, furthermore, a performer on that most romantic of instruments, the harp, gave them not a moment's concern, which is confirmation that their very considerable vanity had not 'taken a musical turn'. If it had, they would not have been so complaisant about Mary's prowess as a harpist or so anxious to have her join them in the then popular pastime of glee singing. It was, of course, lucky that Miss Crawford, though a 'sweet, pretty girl', was small, dark-eyed and brown-complexioned. The Miss Bertrams were 'too handsome themselves to dislike any other woman for being so', but only, it seems, if she was not 'tall, full formed and fair'. Had Mary's attractions been like their own 'it would have been more of a trial'.

The first mention of Mary Crawford's harp occurs when she tells Edmund of its imminent arrival at Mansfield:

> 'Mr Bertram . . . I have had tidings of my harp at last. I am assured that it is safe at Northampton; and there it has probably been these ten days, in spite of the solemn assurances we have so often received to the contrary.'
>
> (*Mansfield Park*, p. 57)

Miss Crawford then complains of the 'piece of work' which has been made about her request for a horse and cart to be diverted from the business of bringing in the hay to the transport of her harp from Northampton, and her astonishment that the haymakers' needs should be given priority over her convenience. Her words are cunningly used to contrast her mercenary standards (although she smiles as she quotes the London maxim that 'everything is to be got by money', it nevertheless condemns her) with the probity and 'sturdy independence' of country life. Edmund gently tries to set her right:

> 'You could not be expected to have thought on the subject before, but when you *do* think of it, you must see the importance of getting in the grass . . . it must be quite out of [the farmers'] power to spare a horse.'
>
> (*Mansfield Park*, p. 58)

This episode is not only used to illustrate the cash-consciousness of the high society world which has made Mary what she is; it also hints that Edmund, despite his own integrity, will soon become too infatuated to take note of the irremediable flaws in Mary's character which remain evident to Fanny.

Though Mary Crawford finds Edmund interesting, and honours his transparent goodness of heart, so different from anything she has previously encountered among the young men of her acquaintance, she cannot adjust herself to his serious conversational manner. Her talk is amusing, at times even witty, but it is too often imbued with an element of frivolity and flirtation which does her some disservice with the reader. It is quite different in tone from the equally lively, but always innocent raillery of Elizabeth Bennet. There are times, too, when Mary, striving to be arch, becomes downright foolish. She cannot even round off the history of her harp's adventures without throwing in a redundant query which is meant to sound gay but is merely silly:

> 'I am to have my harp fetched tomorrow. Henry . . . has offered to fetch it in his barouche. Will it not be honourably conveyed?'
>
> (*Mansfield Park*, pp. 58–59)

Such a question does not deserve a reply and Edmund passes it over. He speaks instead of the harp as his favourite instrument, hoping to hear Miss Crawford play it soon, and Fanny, who has never heard the harp, echoes him. Miss Crawford says she will be most happy to play to them both:

> '. . . at least as long as you can like to listen; probably longer, for I dearly love music myself, and where the natural taste is equal, the player must always be best off, for she is gratified in more ways than one.'
>
> (*Mansfield Park*, p. 59)

Though it is not perfectly clear to me what she means by the 'natural taste' being 'equal', Miss Crawford appears to show another side of herself with this speech – an obliging, modest (one assumes, at least, that she means to be modest about her playing), pleasant side which, like

others of her fairly numerous virtues, is 'only too becoming'. But then she flies off again into her arch, over-
lively style:

> 'Now Mr Bertram, if you write to your brother, I
> entreat you to tell him my harp *is* come, he heard so
> much of my misery without it. And you may say, if you
> please, that I shall prepare my most plaintive airs
> against his return, in compassion to his feelings, as I
> know his horse will lose.'

There is a sting in the tail of this last remark, for Mary
had earlier decided that Tom Bertram – good-looking,
heir to a baronetcy and with the reversion of a splendid
property to look forward to – would do for her very well.
But it had soon become clear that Tom, superficial and
dissipated, had 'no thoughts of marrying at present',
the pleasures of gambling and sporting life in the company
of other young bloods being more to his taste than idle
flirting with Mary Crawford. So off he went to B - - - - - -
to watch his horse win (as he hoped) its race, and, by
doing so, save him from another disagreeable interview
with his father about his mounting debts.

Miss Crawford could not quite forgive Tom Bertram
his indifference to her charms, but she was soon reconciled
to his absence, for she found Edmund's conversation and
evident admiration so greatly to her liking that were the
older brother 'now to step forward the owner of Mansfield
Park, the Sir Thomas complete which he was to be in
time, she did not believe she could accept him.' The
arrival, at long last, of her harp put the finishing touch to
Miss Crawford's manifold attractions:

> . . . for she played with the greatest obligingness, with an
> expression and taste which were peculiarly becoming,
> and there was something clever to be said at the close of
> every air. Edmund was at the parsonage every day to be
> indulged with his favourite instrument; one morning
> secured an invitation for the next, for the lady could not
> be unwilling to have a listener, and everything was soon
> in fair train.

A young woman, pretty, lively, with a harp as elegant as herself; and both placed near a window cut
down to the ground, and opening on a little lawn,
surrounded by shrubs in all the rich foliage of summer,
was enough to catch any man's heart . . . it was all in
harmony.

(*Mansfield Park*, pp. 64–5)

It was all harmony at the parsonage, but at Mansfield
Park Fanny's troubled heart beat with the painful,
monotonous throb of jealousy. She tried to tell herself
that it was natural for Edmund to wish to hear the harp
every morning – 'she would gladly have gone there too,
might she have gone uninvited and unnoticed . . .' – but
it would not do. True, she *did* want to hear the harp –
she had said so when the instrument was first mentioned,
though Miss Crawford seemed not to remember it – but
I think she wanted much more to keep a watch on
Edmund's growing preoccupation with the fair performer,
even though such observation could only bring her an
increase of pain and sorrow. Mary Crawford's harp is,
indeed, a vital factor in the development of Edmund's
passion for her, since it allows him an excuse to spend all
his mornings in her company (chaperoned, of course, by
her sister, Mrs Grant), and it is the frequency and intimacy
of these meetings which brings the emotions of them both
to a climax. Jane Austen has further uses for Mary's
harp before her tale is done, but first Fanny must suffer
from the effect of another of Mary's musical talents.

The scene is the drawing-room of Mansfield Park at
twilight. Edmund stands with Mary and Fanny at an open
window, looking out on to the darkening garden. They
discuss first the expected return from the West Indies
of Sir Thomas Bertram, and then Maria's forthcoming
marriage to Mr Rushworth, turning, as they do, to look
at Maria, seated at the pianoforte, with her fiancé and
Henry Crawford (the man she really loves) both engaged
in arranging candles on the instrument for her. Fanny has
little to say at first, but Mary has a good deal, once the

subject of the clergy arises. There is an important exchange between her and Edmund which makes clear the depth of their disagreement on a matter vital to them both – his future profession. But before either of them can say anything to regret, Mary is 'earnestly invited by the Miss Bertrams to join them in a glee':

> . . . she tripped off to the instrument, leaving Edmund looking after her in an ecstasy of admiration of all her many virtues.
>
> (*Mansfield Park*, p. 112)

It is the first mention of Mary Crawford as a singer, but as most of Jane Austen's young ladies sing as well as play it can be no surprise to us that Mary is equipped to collaborate with the Miss Bertrams in the now forgotten drawing-room amusement of glee-singing.

With Miss Crawford thus occupied, the field is, for once, clear for Fanny, and she has the pleasure of seeing Edmund continue at the window with her in spite of the expected glee. She rhapsodises rather sentimentally about the beauty of the night and the stars and expresses a wish that she could see Cassiopeia. Edmund, to her delight, suggests that they should go together into the garden; he agrees that it is a great while since they have had any star-gazing. '. . . I do not know how it has happened'. Fanny knows, only too well. They are on the point of going out when the glee begins:

> 'We will stay till this is finished, Fanny,' said he, turning his back on the window; and as it advanced, she had the mortification of seeing him advance too, moving forward by gentle degrees towards the instrument, and when it ceased, he was close by the singers, among the most urgent in requesting to hear the glee again.
>
> (*Mansfield Park*, p. 113)

Once more it is music which has drawn Edmund away from Fanny into the radius of Mary's charm, and which now holds him in her thrall, as if within the confines of a magic circle.

But the pleasures of glee-singing at Mansfield Park now give place to the headier delights of private theatricals; and, as is so often the case in amateur dramatic companies, all sorts of simmering passions are soon brought to boiling-point. For Fanny's is not the only troubled heart among the group of young people assembled there to rehearse Mrs Inchbald's very inferior play, *Lovers' Vows,* in which there is no scene even a quarter as dramatic as the unexpected return of Sir Thomas Bertram in the midst of one of the final rehearsals. This event precipitates several crises of which the baronet himself remains quite oblivious:

> The evening passed with external smoothness, though almost every mind was ruffled; and the music which Sir Thomas called for from his daughters helped to conceal the want of real harmony.
>
> *(Mansfield Park,* p. 191)

Sir Thomas's return is a signal for a gradual dispersal of most of the young people. Maria marries Mr Rushworth and they leave for a honeymoon in Brighton, accompanied by their chief bridesmaid, Julia (a strange custom of the period), and now, with the Bertram sisters gone, Fanny and Miss Crawford are thrown more together. Feeling as she does about Mary, Fanny would not have sought her out as a companion, but a wet day obliges Fanny to take shelter in the parsonage and at last she has an opportunity to hear the harp:

> It was beginning to look brighter, when Fanny, observing a harp in the room, asked some questions about it, which soon led to an acknowledgement of her wishing very much to hear it, and a confession, which could hardly be believed, of her never yet having heard it since its being in Mansfield . . . Miss Crawford, calling to mind an early-expressed wish on the subject, was concerned at her own neglect; – and 'shall I play to you now?' – and 'what will you have?' were questions immediately following with the readiest good humour.
>
> She played accordingly; happy to have a new listener,

and a listener who seemed so much obliged, so full of
wonder at the performance, and who showed herself not
wanting in taste.

(*Mansfield Park*, pp. 206–7)

One would like to know just how Fanny showed herself
to possess that musical taste of which we have heard so
much and will hear yet more. Was it revealed by her
appreciative words about 'the wonder of the performance'?
No, for, as we shall see, Jane Austen will later make a
distinction between 'execution' and 'taste'. It appears that
the word may have had more than one interpretation,
and that in the case of a good listener, such as Fanny, it
may merely have meant that her musical preferences
happened to coincide with those of the performer.

Fanny, beginning to feel uneasy about staying too long,
prepares to go, but Miss Crawford detains her:

> 'Another quarter of an hour . . . And besides, I want
> to play something more to you – a very pretty piece –
> and your cousin Edmund's prime favourite. You must
> stay and hear your cousin's favourite.'
> Fanny felt that she must . . . and she fancied him
> sitting in that room, listening with constant delight to
> the favourite air, played, as it appeared to her, with
> superior tone and expression; and though pleased with
> it herself, and glad to like whatever was liked by him,
> she was more sincerely impatient to go away at the
> conclusion of it than she had even been before.

(*Mansfield Park*, p. 207)

It would have required a more experienced listener than
Fanny to detect anything so subtle as 'superior tone and
expression' in the performance of 'a very pretty piece'
played on the harp. It is merely the association of the
music with the absent beloved which allows Fanny (and
Jane Austen) to imagine a difference in Mary's playing
of it, but it serves its purpose by filling Fanny's mind with
confused emotions and with an urgent desire to get away
from Mary as soon as possible.

The next important event is a dinner party at the

parsonage during which Mary overhears Dr Grant advis-
ing Edmund about the living he is to take up once he has
been ordained. She realises that her expressed disapprobation of the church as a profession has not yet swayed
Edmund in his resolve to proceed with ordination, and
this so much angers her that she becomes quite unsociable:

> . . . Miss Crawford took her harp, . . . [Fanny] had
> nothing to do but to listen . . . Miss Crawford was too
> much vexed by what had passed to be in a humour for
> anything but music. With that, she soothed herself and
> amused her friend.
>
> (*Mansfield Park*, p. 227)

There is considerable irony in Jane Austen's use of the
word 'friend' here. It is only Mary Crawford who, at this
point in the story, flatters herself that Fanny is her friend.
Fanny is, of course, no such thing. Indeed it would hardly
be overstating the case to call her Mary's enemy.

The ball at Mansfield Park now takes place, and this
memorable occasion is quickly followed by the departure
of the young men of the party, leaving Fanny alone at the
Park with her uncle and aunts, and Mary Crawford
disconsolate at the parsonage. Mary, though extremely
piqued that Edmund has gone to Peterborough to be
ordained, feels his absence acutely and becomes a prey
to an emotion new to her, though not to Fanny – the
unpleasant emotion of jealousy. She begins to imagine that
Edmund's absence, prolonged beyond the expected week,
might be on account of the charms of one or other of the
Miss Owens, sisters of the friend with whom he is staying.
Unable to endure being quite without news of the man she
now freely acknowledges to herself that she loves, she makes
her way through the muddy lanes of a wet January morning to Mansfield Park, where she questions Fanny
about the Miss Owens, as unaware that she is giving
herself away with every word she says as of Fanny's true
feelings for Edmund:

'How many Miss Owens are there?'

'Three grown up.'

'Are they musical?'

'I do not know at all. I never heard.'

'That is the first question, you know,' said Miss Crawford, trying to appear gay and unconcerned, 'which every woman who plays herself is sure to ask about another. But it is very foolish to ask questions about any young ladies – about any three sisters just grown up; for one knows, without being told, exactly what they are – all very accomplished and pleasing, and *one* very pretty. There is a beauty in every family. – It is the regular thing. Two play on the piano-forte, and one on the harp – and all sing – or would sing if they were taught – or sing all the better for not being taught – or something like it.'

> *(Mansfield Park, p. 288)*

Mary Crawford's anxiety over the possible musical accomplishments of the Miss Owens makes clear that she regards her own harp-playing as an important weapon in her sexual armoury, and so reveals another facet of her essentially worldly character. It also supports the theory of certain leading Jane Austen scholars that she is a sister beneath the skin, and perhaps directly derived from the unpleasant Lady Susan, that most mercenary of Jane Austen's women, whose views on the importance of musical accomplishments in young women as a snare for the opposite sex have already been quoted.[22]

Though the scene in which Mary Crawford pumps Fanny about the Miss Owens occurs only towards the end of the second volume of *Mansfield Park*, and there is still the whole of Volume Three for the development and climax of the story, the tide has already turned in Fanny's favour, though she does not know it. Jane Austen has no further use for Mary's harp, and after its owner's return to London we never see it or her again, though we read, with the recipient's eyes, the extremely foolish and always overly-arch letters which Mary wrote to Fanny while the latter was staying in Portsmouth. The last part of the novel gradually unfolds to a dramatic – even a slightly

melodramatic – dénouement, culminating in the, to me,
not entirely credible elopement of Maria Rushworth with
Henry Crawford. These final pages of *Mansfield Park*
are thought by many critics to be on a somewhat lower
level of inspiration than the rest of the work (it remains,
however, one of the greatest novels in the English
language), and, if this is true, the reason probably lies
in the fact that it took the authoress a little outside the
limits of her personal experience – limits which she never
transgressed elsewhere. It brought her face to face with
'guilt and misery', the discussion of which she preferred
to leave to 'other pens'. Fortunately it is not necessary
for my pen to deal with 'such odious subjects' for the third
volume of *Mansfield Park* contains no mention of music.

CHAPTER VIII

Emma

IN NO other novel did Jane Austen find more important or varied uses for music than in *Emma*. Furthermore, the values which she had placed upon the art in *Pride and Prejudice* are, in the later work, interestingly reversed, Emma Woodhouse's modest attainments being rated, quite properly, a long way below the very finished musical performances of Jane Fairfax. Miss Fairfax, though a skilled musician, is (unlike poor Mary Bennet) beautiful, elegant and intellectually superior in spite of her poverty, while Emma, equally handsome and intelligent but also rich, is made to feel guilty over the relative inferiority of her own playing and singing.

A distinguished Jane Austen scholar has observed that the extremely complex plot of *Emma* is, among many other things, a detective story.[23] It is a detective story, moreover, for which the authoress, playing as scrupulously fair with her readers as would a Sayers or a Simenon, provides a trail of carefully laid clues which, if correctly interpreted, can lead one straight to the solution of the mystery of why Jane Fairfax elected to share the 'confined circumstances' and the extremely narrow social horizon of her Highbury relations, the Bateses, when she might have gone with her benefactors, the Campbells, to enjoy a season of luxury and gaiety among the Irish Ascendency. It is Emma's misinterpretation of these clues which provides this most perfect of Jane Austen's works with one of its principal themes, and which adds many subtle touches to the wonderful portrait of a wrong-headed and extremely fallible heroine who is, nevertheless (such is Jane Austen's

77

great art), convincingly 'faultless in spite of all her faults'.

The most important clue to the reason for Jane Fairfax's visit to her grandmother and aunt is the mysterious arrival of a pianoforte at Mrs Bates's humble home. The subsequent discussions of this event by the principal characters are used by the authoress to reveal their thoughts about themselves and about each other, and also to advance the story. Emma's misplaced confidence in her own perspicacity; Frank Churchill's high spirits and occasional selfishness; Jane's embarrassment and tortured conscience (her secret engagement to Frank must, it appears, be regarded as a very serious impropriety), and Mr Knightley's mature judgment and acute observation (he alone sees that the unknown giver of the pianoforte has made its recipient a subject for gossip) are all developed in conversation, while the scene in Mrs Bates's little sitting-room, where most of the principal characters are brought together to admire the new instrument, is unsurpassed and, indeed, hardly equalled elsewhere in Jane Austen's work for the cobweb-like intricacy of its tensions.

It is with the arrival in Highbury of Jane Fairfax that music comes to the fore in *Emma*, but the subject is introduced much earlier in the book, and in such a way that the reader is already prepared for Emma's chagrin when, eventually, her amateurish playing is compared with, and placed in the shade by, Jane's near-professional brilliance. The very first mention of music in *Emma* is, however, quite unconnected with either of the young ladies' abilities: it occurs in a conversation between Emma and her protegée, Harriet Smith, and it touches on a very unusual subject for Jane Austen's time – that of folk-singing. Harriet has been giving Emma an account of her visit during the previous summer to the home of a young farmer, Robert Martin, who is in love with her:

'. . . he was so very obliging! He had his shepherd's son into the parlour one night on purpose to sing to her. She was very fond of singing. He could sing a little himself.' (*Emma*, p. 28)

Pretty, plump and very ignorant, Harriet knows nothing of music. Her pleasure in the untaught singing of the shepherd's son is all of a piece with the artless simplicity of her character. English folk songs, sung unaccompanied, would have appealed to her at least as much for the stories they told as for the beauty of their ancient melodies. Jane Austen's was not an age when folk music was valued by polite society (despite the contemporary fashion for 'Scotch songs' and 'Irish melodies'), and Harriet's account of the musical entertainment provided for her at Abbey Mill Farm will have amused Emma and also pleased her as evidence of her little friend's unformed taste and general need for 'improvement'. No doubt Mr Martin's own repertoire of songs was as small as his collection of books (which, according to Harriet, consisted only of *The Vicar of Wakefield*, *Elegant Extracts* and the *Agricultural Reports*), and, like that of his shepherd's boy, limited to traditional airs, sung unaccompanied, for it is improbable that the Martins owned any sort of keyboard instrument. Though the daughters of the family had, like Harriet, been to Mrs Goddard's school in Highbury there is no mention that any of that lady's forty pupils ('. . . a train of twenty young couple . . . walked after her to church.') were taught to play the pianoforte. Their education was evidently quite rudimentary and certainly Harriet's was concluded without her having acquired any artistic accomplishments. To Harriet, Emma's unpractised playing and mediocre singing seemed wonderful indeed, but the reader soon learns the truth of the matter, and it proves revelatory not only of Emma's character and artistic limitations but of the general lack of any critical standard in Highbury society:

> She had always wanted to do everything, and had made more progress both in drawing and music than many might have done with so little labour as she would ever submit to. She played and sang . . . but steadiness had always been wanting; and in nothing had she approached the degree of excellence which she would have

been glad to command, and ought not to have failed
of. She was not much deceived as to her own skill . . .
but she was not unwilling to have others deceived, or
sorry to know her reputation for accomplishment often
higher than it deserved.

(Emma, p. 44)

With this passage the authoress adds many details to the
evolving portrait of her heroine. We see Emma as versatile
and gifted but sadly lacking in application. She was without illusions about her failure to make the best use of her
gifts: she was self-satisfied about a good many things but
never about her appearance or her accomplishments,
though quite ready to accept admiration and praise which
she knew to be unmerited.

Despite her life of comfort and security, one has some
reason to feel sorry for Emma. She needed the guidance of
a firmer hand than Miss Taylor's. Having lost her mother
early, and with an elderly father (Mr Woodhouse had not
married young) whose total abdication from responsibility
left her free to do exactly as she pleased, she was really
out of luck in that her governess, though a motherly,
warm-hearted woman and one who really loved her
charge, was as wax in the hands of so strong-willed a
pupil. And Miss Taylor, obviously no disciplinarian, does
not appear to have been much of an educationalist either.
Her duties would have included instruction in drawing and
music, as well in the supervision of Emma's reading, but
she had no reason to congratulate herself on her pupil's
progress in any of these subjects. Mr Knightley's frank
assessment of Emma's virtues and failings – the unfortunate lack of application which counteracted her natural
gifts and bright intelligence – was quickly recognised by
her former governess as a criticism of her own work as a
teacher ('I should have been sorry, Mr Knightley, to be
dependent on *your* recommendation, had I quitted Mr
Woodhouse's family and wanted another situation . . .'),
but the probability is that, despite her profession until her
marriage to Mr Weston, Miss Taylor's own artistic

accomplishments were not at all remarkable. Though she will have conscientiously taught Emma all she knew about music it cannot have been very much. For what do we hear of Miss Taylor's, or rather Mrs Weston's musical powers? We are told that she was 'capital in her country dances', which at least suggests that her playing had a good rhythmic pulse to it, but there is never any occasion when she is called upon to play anything more demanding than dance music. The Coles, having purchased a new grand pianoforte, are 'in hopes that Miss Woodhouse will be prevailed upon to try it', but it does not occur to them to invite Miss Woodhouse's teacher, Mrs Weston, to do likewise. The fuss about the arrival of Jane Fairfax's pianoforte involves most of Highbury society, and we learn that Mrs Weston, 'kind-hearted and musical', was particularly interested in the circumstances and had much to ask and to say 'as to tone, touch and pedal'. But in spite of her interest she had to sit quietly by and listen to the owner's (admittedly excellent) playing, for no one thought of suggesting that she might like to try the instrument herself.

It seems unlikely, therefore, that Mrs Weston had any great reputation as a pianist in Highbury; which leads one to suspect that the lack of polish in her pupil's playing may not have been entirely Emma's own fault. Without the sound technical foundation which can only come from good teaching, her spasmodic bouts of practising must, inevitably, have led to discouragement and frustration; and though it was characteristic of her to blame herself alone we cannot leave out of account the probable shortcomings of her teacher.

However, during the opening chapters of the novel, Emma has very little time to repine about her musical deficiencies; she is too much occupied by her schemes for detaching Harriet from Farmer Martin and marrying her off to Mr Elton, the ambitious and somewhat affected young vicar of Highbury. It takes an excited announcement by Miss Bates that Jane Fairfax will soon be among them again to renew in Emma the sense of irritation which

the idea of Jane has always produced in the past, but
which in moments of honesty with herself, she allows to be
largely the result of her envy of Jane's superior
accomplishments.

Emma has never liked Jane, and Miss Bates bores her to
distraction, but this does not prevent her from inviting
them both, with old Mrs Bates, to an evening party at
Hartfield as soon as possible after Jane's arrival. On all
occasions where polite social behaviour and a 'sense of
what is right' are required, Emma knows what to do, and
if we are to impute some of her weaknesses to her former
governess's pedagogical inadequacy it is only fair to
allow Mrs Weston a share of credit for the grace and good
manners with which Emma invariably does the honours
of her father's house.

Unfortunately Emma's good resolution – to try to like
Jane Fairfax more than formerly – is not lasting:

> They had music; Emma was obliged to play; and the
> thanks and praise which necessarily followed appeared
> to her an affectation of candour, an air of greatness,
> meaning only to show off in higher style her own very
> superior performance.
>
> (*Emma*, pp. 168–9)

Emma is being quite irrational here: Jane could hardly
have done otherwise than praise her hostess's performance
– her manners were at least as good as Emma's – and it is
'uncandid' of Emma to criticise her guest for not telling her
the unvarnished truth. But she is, of course, right to think
that Jane lacks 'candour' in other respects, for the latter
has something to hide and is, therefore, all caution and
reserve. She is particularly reticent on the subject of Frank
Churchill, the son by a first marriage of that very Mr
Weston who has recently married Emma's beloved Miss
Taylor. Emma has a lively curiosity about Frank, whom
she has never seen, but her persistent questioning of Jane
Fairfax (she knows that Frank and Jane have met at
Weymouth) gets her nowhere. Finding Jane's non-

committal replies 'repulsive', Emma allows irritation to cloud her judgment, and perversely misinterprets Jane's polite praise of her playing. Perhaps it might have been better if Emma had withstood the requests of her guests and not played at all in her own drawing-room, contenting herself merely with 'opening the instrument' for Jane, as Charlotte Lucas had done for Elizabeth in *Pride and Prejudice*. But at least she played a good deal less than her guest, or so it seems from Mr Knightley's remarks during a call at Hartfield on the morning after the party:

> 'A very pleasant evening . . . You and Miss Fairfax gave us some very good music. I do not know a more luxurious state . . . than sitting at one's ease to be entertained a whole evening by two such young women; sometimes with music and sometimes with conversation . . . I was glad you made her play so much, for having no instrument at her grandmother's, it must have been a real indulgence.'
>
> (*Emma*, p. 170)

As is so often the case with a seemingly unimportant speech by one of Jane Austen's characters, this one tells us something about the speaker himself and gives us a good deal of information besides. Mr Knightley must be quite well aware that Emma's music-making is not very good, but, though he is perhaps the only person in her admiring circle who never flatters her, he diplomatically avoids hurting her *amour propre* and praises her performance and Jane's as if they were of equal merit. He is aware of Emma's feelings about Jane Fairfax and he is anxious for the two girls to be on better terms, being concerned for the welfare of both. He is worried about Emma's growing intimacy with Harriet Smith, which he thinks unwise – 'a bad thing', he calls it – and he would like to see it superseded by a closer relationship with Jane, who is Emma's equal in age and intelligence. He is also concerned for Jane, knowing her to be a little unwell and in need of relief from her aunt's incessant chatter and her grandmother's cramped apartment. Lastly we learn from him that old Mrs Bates does not own a pianoforte, and thus the way is prepared for the eventual arrival of the mysterious instrument from Broadwood's.

Frank Churchill is such an important character in *Emma*, and his romance with Jane Fairfax such a strong motif in the complex pattern of plot and counter-plot, that it is something of a surprise to note that he does not make his appearance until the fifth chapter of the second volume of the novel. Once arrived in Highbury, however, he compensates for his late entry by a good deal of activity and much lively conversation with Emma, and the more he talks the clearer his engaging, if wilful, personality becomes to the reader.

Like all lovers, Frank feels impelled to bring his in-amorata's name into the conversation as often as possible, and few of his exchanges with Emma pass without Jane's being discussed. Quite ignorant of their secret engagement, Emma incautiously says a number of things about Miss Fairfax which later she must blush to remember. Frank is amused and wickedly leads her on, but while he is drawing the wool over her eyes as to the real situation he unintentionally gives her new material for an absurd fantasy which her fertile imagination had earlier evolved about a possible romance between Jane and a Mr Dixon, the husband of Jane's great friend, the former Miss Campbell. In the course of a discussion of Jane's outstanding musical ability, Frank provides Emma with what seems to be a corroboration of her suspicions:

'Did you ever hear the young lady we were speaking of, play?' said Frank Churchill.

'Ever hear her!' repeated Emma. 'You forget how much she belongs to Highbury. I have heard her every year of our lives since we both began. She plays charmingly.'

'You think so, do you? – I wanted the opinion of some one who could really judge. She appeared to me to play well, that is, with considerable taste, but I know nothing of the matter myself. – I am excessively fond of

music, but without the smallest skill or right of judging
of any body's performance. – I have been used to hear
her's admired; and I remember one proof of her being
thought to play well: – a man, a very musical man, and
in love with another woman – engaged to her – on the
point of marriage – would yet never ask that other
woman to sit down to the instrument, if the lady in
question could sit down instead – never seemed to like
to hear one if he could hear the other. That I thought,
in a man of known musical talent, was some proof.'

'Proof, indeed!' said Emma, highly amused. – 'Mr
Dixon is very musical, is he? . . .'

(Emma, pp. 201–2)

Frank cannot deny that Mr Dixon and Miss Campbell
were the persons concerned, whereupon Emma, delighted
by what she regards as proof positive that her guess-work
has been accurate, shocks us by imparting to her companion her conjecture that Miss Fairfax has a guilty
secret – which, of course, she has, though not the one
Emma has in mind. Emma really behaves very badly,
for she allows her animus against Jane to become much too
apparent. It is one of those occasions when one feels
ashamed of Emma and longs to give her a hint, *sotto
voce*, to change the subject – to talk of books or music, or
even 'to speak with exquisite calmness and gravity of the
weather', as she was once obliged to do in an awkward
moment. Anything would be better than for her to blunder
on in such an uncharitable manner, and with such
unreserve, to a young man she hardly knows, but who
knows the truth about the persons she is discussing and
who is laughing at her up his sleeve.

Frank is, of course, being very devious. He has Emma
at a disadvantage and he has led her into a trap. He really
had no reason, other than the pleasure of talking of his
beloved, to ask for her judgment of Jane's playing, which
he knew very well to be excellent and which he was capable
of judging for himself. For though he disclaimed any sort
of musical ability, he was not telling the truth, as was to

become evident a few days later at the Coles' party.
His pride in, and admiration for, Jane's playing is, in fact,
so strong that it now inspires in him the idea of giving her
what he knows she misses most at her grandmother's – a
pianoforte. His action is as misguided as it is impulsive and
generous, for it quite disregards the embarrassments
which such a valuable and anonymous gift could cause
its recipient. Frank makes the rather feeble excuse to his
father and step-mother that he must go to London to
get his hair cut. He dashes up to town, where he doubtless
visits his barber before going straight on to Broadwood's
establishment in Great Pulteney Street, there to select
the best square pianoforte in stock. He then buys some of
the latest pianoforte music (sheet music could also be
obtained at Broadwood's) and orders the whole to be
despatched to Highbury as soon as possible.

The extravagance of Frank's gift should not be overlooked. A very similar instrument to that which he presented to his fiancée – a square pianoforte of five and a
half octaves, made by Broadwood in 1815 – can be seen
in the Colt Clavier Collection at Benenden, in Kent.
It is an elegant piece of workmanship. It is made of
mahogany and decorated with inlay and ormolu, and it
has small integral drawers for the storage of music. A
comparable instrument would have cost Frank between
twenty and thirty guineas (Rosamund Harding, in her
important book, *The Piano-Forte*, mentions £26 as the
current price for an 'elegant' Broadwood square pianoforte in 1815), to which must be added the music sent with
it and the delivery charges. The value of such a gift was
probably not much less than a quarter of old Mrs Bates's
entire annual income. No wonder the pianoforte's unexpected arrival caused a sensation in Highbury. It also
gives us an idea of the liberality of Frank's allowance from
the Churchills, the uncle and aunt who had made him
their heir and whose name he had adopted.

The pianoforte is first mentioned by Mrs Cole, a minor
character who is useful to the authoress for conveying

information. The Coles are rich, but being 'in trade' they are Emma's social inferiors. They give a grand dinner party at which, after much initial indecision and misgiving, Emma graciously condescends to be present. It is while the guests are assembling in the drawing-room before dinner that Mrs Cole relates how she has been calling on Miss Bates that afternoon (how did she find time amid the preparations for her party?) and has seen with astonishment the mysterious and splendid pianoforte. According to Mrs Cole, the Bateses and Jane are all equally at a loss to know whose gift it is, and can only conjecture that it is a present from Colonel Campbell. Jane, of course, knows well enough who sent it. Mrs Cole has much to say:

'1 declare, I do not know when 1 have heard anything that has given me more satisfaction! – It always has quite hurt me that Jane Fairfax, who plays so delightfully, should not have an instrument. It seemed quite a shame, especially considering how many houses there are where fine instruments are absolutely thrown away. This is like giving ourselves a slap, to be sure! and it was but yesterday I was telling Mr Cole, I really was ashamed to look at our new grand pianoforté in the drawing-room, while I do not know one note from another, and our little girls, who are just beginning, perhaps may never make anything of it; and there is poor Jane Fairfax, who is mistress of music, has not anything of the nature of an instrument, not even the pitifullest old spinnet in the world, to amuse herself with. – I was saying this to Mr Cole but yesterday, and he quite agreed with me; only he is so particularly fond of music that he could not help indulging himself in the purchase, hoping that some of our good neighbours might be so obliging occasionally to put it to a better use than we can; and that really is the reason why the instrument was bought – or else I am sure we ought to be ashamed of it. – We are in great hopes that Miss Woodhouse may be prevailed with to try it this evening.'
Miss Woodhouse made the proper acquiescence.

(*Emma*, p. 215)

A striking example of the class snobbery of Jane Austen's time is illustrated by the composition of Mrs Cole's list of guests for her dinner party. The Coles, though rich, are considered to be only 'moderately genteel'. They are social climbers, and their party is planned as an important step in their progress up the ladder of Highbury society, at the top of which Emma Woodhouse reigns supreme. They are, however, rather unsure of themselves, and they realise that they risk a rebuff, so they go about the matter with great circumspection. Probably for reasons of business they are obliged to invite the lawyer, Mr Cox, and his eldest son, but it is significant that the invitation does not extend to the female part of the Cox family. Mrs Cole may well have heard that Emma considers the Miss Coxes to be 'without exception, the most vulgar girls in Highbury'. Other than the Mr Coxes, however, the guests are nearly all Emma's particular friends – the Westons, Frank Churchill and Mr Knightley – the only addition being one 'unexceptionable country [for country, read county[24]] family whom the Coles have the advantage of naming among their acquaintance'. It seems very likely that the 'unexceptionable' people were a Mr and Mrs Gilbert who are mentioned, a few days later, during a discussion at Randalls, the home of the Westons, as having been present at the Coles' party. The invitation to the Woodhouses is held back until everyone else's acceptance has been received so that Emma may become aware of exactly who will be present at the dinner. But with all her care and forethought, Mrs Cole cannot have been entirely happy about the final arrangement of her table. Eleven is an extremely awkward number for a dinner party, and while it is true that Mr Woodhouse, had he consented to be present, would have brought it up to a round dozen, the preponderance of men over women, already much too large, would then have been greater still. So far, however, there is nothing to which we may take particular exception, unless it is the exclusion of Mrs and the Miss Coxes. But when dinner is over and the ladies adjourn to the drawing-room, various other, less exalted members of Highbury society begin to make their appearance, among them Miss Bates, Jane Fairfax and Harriet Smith, all of whom, it seems, are quite content to swell the party to a respectable size and, in the case of Jane Fairfax, to perform for the entertainment of the more important guests, in return for cups of tea and light refreshments. One would like to believe that such distinctions, invidiously based on wealth, are entirely a thing of the remote past. Perhaps they may be, but I am not fully convinced that these and similar snobbish practices, very prevalent in the Highburys of Jane Austen's England, are totally unknown in our own time.

Inevitably the moment comes when music is called for:

> . . . a little bustle in the room shewed them that tea was over, and the instrument in preparation; – and at the same moment Mr Cole approaching to entreat Miss Woodhouse would do them the honour of trying it . . . and as, in every respect, it suited Emma best to lead, she gave a very proper compliance.
>
> She knew the limitations of her own powers too well to attempt more than she could perform with credit; she wanted neither taste nor spirit in the little things which are generally acceptable, and could accompany her own voice well. One accompaniment to her song took her agreeably by surprize – a second, slightly but correctly taken by Frank Churchill. Her pardon was duly begged at the close of the song, and every thing usual followed. He was accused of having a delightful voice, and a perfect knowledge of music; which was properly denied; and that he knew nothing of the matter, and had no voice at all, roundly asserted. They sang together once more; and Emma would then resign her place to Miss Fairfax, whose performance, both vocal and instrumental, she never could attempt to conceal from herself, was infinitely superior to her own.
>
> (*Emma*, p. 227)

The observant reader will have noted something which escaped Emma: that Frank Churchill cannot always be

relied upon to speak the exact truth. He had earlier
pretended that he was 'without the smallest skill in music',
but now we find him joining in her song with an obbligato
which appears to have been improvised on the spur of the
moment. And though he modestly disclaimed the 'perfect
knowledge of music' with which he was publicly credited
as soon as the song ended, it is obvious that he knew more
about the matter than he would allow. He certainly
showed no reluctance to perform (was he even a trifle
conceited about his vocal powers?), for when Emma
obliged her audience for a second time Frank joined in
once more. Of course he had an ulterior motive for singing
with Emma: he was only waiting for the moment when
Jane would replace her at the keyboard – when he and his
betrothed would sing together, 'the sweet sounds of [their]
united voices' expressing symbolically that unity in marriage to which they both looked forward. We are here
reminded of the duets sung by Marianne Dashwood with
Willoughby; for their love affair, too, though not 'illicit'
in quite the same way as Jane's with Frank, was a thing
never openly acknowledged.

Meanwhile Emma, having performed 'with taste and
spirit' one or two 'little things' from her repertoire, moves
some distance away from the instrument and prepares to
listen to Jane's 'superior' performance 'with mixed
feelings'. Frank and Jane sing together. It comes out that
they have sung duets once or twice before, at Weymouth,
but nobody suspects that this might imply a rather closer
intimacy than the quite superficial acquaintanceship
which is all that they have admitted to; for as Frank has
had the forethought to use Emma as a blind it seems natural enough that he should sing with Jane as well.

Mr Knightley now sits by Emma and they embark on a
lively conversation, regardless of the fact that the singers
are still delighting the company. He speaks with warm
admiration of Jane's performance, and then they touch
on other matters, among them Jane's new pianoforte.
Mr Knightley disapproves of such anonymous gifts –

'surprises are foolish things'. It is odd that Emma and Mr Knightley are allowed to talk while music is being performed and get away with it unscathed. When Sir John Middleton had talked through Marianne's playing, or when Lady Catherine de Bourgh 'listened to half a song, and then talked on, as before' Jane Austen found a means to express strong disapproval of such rudeness. Emma and Mr Knightley, however, appear to have a special dispensation to talk against music, for they escape any kind of censure. Mr Knightley is evidently able to talk and listen at the same time, for it is he who observes that Jane's voice is showing signs of fatigue:

> Towards the end of Jane's second song her voice grew thick.
> 'That will do,' said he, when it was finished, thinking aloud – 'you have sung quite enough for one evening – now, be quiet.'
> Another song, however, was soon begged for . . . Frank Churchill was heard to say, 'I think you could manage this without effort; the first part is so very trifling. The strength of the song falls on the second.'
> Mr Knightley grew angry.
> 'That fellow,' said he, indignantly, 'thinks of nothing but shewing off his own voice. This must not be.' And touching Miss Bates, who at that moment passed near – 'Miss Bates, are you mad, to let your niece sing herself hoarse in this manner? Go, and interfere . . .'
> (*Emma*, p. 229)

It is part of Mr Knightley's personality to be frank and outspoken, but his manner of addressing Miss Bates on this occasion was as near to plain rudeness as makes no matter. Does anyone, least of all one of Jane Austen's gentlemen, speak with such uncalled-for brusqueness as this elsewhere in her novels? Mrs Norris was consistently unkind and frequently said terrible things to Fanny, but they were close relations. Lady Catherine insulted Elizabeth and shouted her down, but she was fighting to save the marriage she had planned between her daughter and Mr

Darcy. Mr Knightley was angry, but with Frank Churchill, not with Miss Bates. It would have been easy for him to have drawn her attention to Jane's condition with a quiet word and a smile, but to attack her with 'are you mad?' was totally unnecessary.

The fact that Jane's voice 'grew thick' after two songs does not speak very well for the soundness of the vocal training she had received in London. No doubt her two songs were very much more ambitious and testing than Emma's 'little things' (they were probably operatic arias, since we are told that she sang in Italian), but, even so, a mere couple of arias should not have made a well-trained singer 'hoarse'. It sounds as if there was something seriously amiss with her method of voice production. And if her songs *were* operatic arias, then Frank's musical attainments must have been even more considerable than one had supposed, since he sang with her, and presumably did so in Italian.

Miss Bates takes no offence at Mr Knightley's commanding tone; she obeys him at once and quickly puts an end to all further singing.

> Here ceased the concert part of the evening, for Miss Woodhouse and Miss Fairfax were the only young-lady-performers; but soon (within five minutes) the proposal of dancing – originating nobody exactly knew where – was so effectually promoted by Mr and Mrs Cole, that every thing was rapidly clearing away, to give proper space. Mrs Weston, capital in her country – dances, was seated, and beginning an irresistible waltz.
> (*Emma*, p. 229)

This is the only time in *Emma* when Mrs Weston plays the pianoforte, and as we have been told that country dances are her special forte, it is initially surprising that she should have led off with a waltz. This seeming anomaly struck G. B. Stern, who thought that perhaps, in 1815, they were somehow able to waltz in sets, like country dancers.[25] Certainly Frank Churchill's 'coming up with most becoming gallantry to Emma' and, after securing her hand, leading her 'up to the top' (that is, to the top of a set), suggests as much. But in fact the waltz, as a dance, though it reached England in 1812, was not yet acceptable in polite society. According to that great authority on the dance, Cecil Sharp, 'the position in which partners were required to engage in the new dance shocked the national sense of propriety and was deemed grossly indecorous'.[26] As there could certainly be no question of Miss Woodhouse, Miss Fairfax or even Miss Smith 'engaging' in positions of *that* nature with their partners (though one can place less reliance on the modesty of the vulgar Miss Coxes, who were among the 'inferior' females invited to put in an appearance during the later part of the evening), what, in fact, did they all dance to the strains of Mrs Weston's irresistible waltz? Cecil Sharp again provides us with the answer:

> Although the dance did not reach us until 1812, numerous Collections of Waltz-airs had been published in England for twenty years or more before that date and used as Country Dance Tunes, furnished with Country Dance figures and called Waltz Country Dances.

Obviously it was some of these tunes which Mrs Weston had ready at her finger tips for the amusement of her young friends, and the movements they performed to them were not the shocking gyrations (with couples closely 'engaged') of the recently imported waltz, but the familiar, old-fashioned figures of the English Country Dance.[27]

Though nothing is said of it, Jane Fairfax, in addition to singing twice, must have played at least one brilliant pianoforte solo at the Coles' party. Mere accompaniments, however well played, would not have thrown Emma into such a mood of despondency over her own performances as we find her in on the morning after the party:

> She did unfeignedly and unequivocally regret the inferiority of her own playing and singing. She did most heartily grieve over the idleness of her childhood – and sat down and practised vigorously an hour and a half.
>
> (*Emma*, p. 231)

The arrival of Harriet while Emma is still practising,
and her exclamation, 'Oh, if I could but play as well as
you and Miss Fairfax!', is an insufficient antidote to
Emma's unwonted mood of self-abasement. She cannot be
consoled by Harriet's uncritical adulation for she knows
it to be founded on ignorance and partiality. The exchanges between them which follow are amusing and
reveal Harriet's stupidity and lack of education as well as
Emma's realism and freedom from personal conceit:

> 'Don't class us together, Harriet. My playing is no
> more like her's, than a lamp is like sunshine.'
> 'Oh! dear – I think you play the best of the two. I
> think you play quite as well as she does. I am sure I had
> much rather hear you. Every body last night said how
> well you played.'
> 'Those who knew any thing about it, must have felt
> the difference. The truth is, Harriet, that my playing is
> just good enough to be praised, but Jane Fairfax's is
> much beyond it.'
> 'Well, I shall always think that you play quite as well
> as she does, or that if there is any difference nobody
> would ever find it out. Mr Cole said how much taste
> you had; and Mr Frank Churchill talked a great deal
> about your taste, and that he valued taste much more
> than execution.'
> 'Ah! but Jane Fairfax has them both, Harriet.'
> 'Are you sure? I saw she had execution, but I did not
> know she had any taste. Nobody talked about it. And I
> hate Italian singing. – There is no understanding a word
> of it.'
>
> (*Emma*, pp. 231–2)

It is time to consider more closely the word 'taste',
which occurs so frequently when music is mentioned in
the novels of Jane Austen. Dr Johnson's various definitions
of taste – sensibility, perception, intellectual relish or
discernment – will have been familiar to her, as will
have been his citation from Swift, who said that to have
taste meant to distinguish intellectually; but Johnson, to
whom music was supremely unimportant, makes no men-

tion of musical taste in his celebrated Dictionary. For Jane Austen, however, it must have been a quality – she obviously considered it to be a very important one – which had little to do with 'execution', that is, with dexterity in performance. It will be recalled that Mary Bennet possessed neither genius nor taste, though she was capable of playing long and technically difficult concertos. At the other extreme, Fanny Price, who could not play at all, was somehow able to show herself to be 'not wanting in taste', though here, I believe, Jane Austen has gone too far, her special affection for Fanny having led her to credit her favourite heroine with a non-existent talent, much as Lady Catherine praised herself and her daughter for possessing musical taste which existed only in her imagination. More to the point is the comparison of Emma Woodhouse's playing, which, as we have just seen, 'wanted neither taste nor spirit' but was rather weak on the side of 'execution', with that of Jane Fairfax, which, on the authority of Emma herself, possessed both qualities in full measure. The difficulty of recognising taste for what it is is most entertainingly illustrated by poor Harriet's assumption that Jane Fairfax did not have it because nobody mentioned it. Even Harriet could see that Jane had 'execution', but taste she was unable to recognise. There is, however, no need to despise Harriet for her ignorance in this matter, as taste is a subtle quality and can only be properly appreciated by those who have it themselves. One might, perhaps, be forgiven for assuming that when Jane Austen wrote of musical taste she merely meant what we mean when we speak of 'feeling' or 'expression' in music. But then we recall that Mary Crawford was described as playing the harp with 'an expression and taste which were peculiarly becoming', and this seems to imply that expression was one thing and taste another – related qualities, perhaps, but not identical ones.

A very early writer on music described genius and taste as 'natural gifts which cannot be learned'.[28] But in the mid-eighteenth century musical 'taste' had acquired another connotation, for we find that Signor Francesco Geminiani's *Rules for Playing in a true Taste on the Violin, German Flute, Violoncello and Harpsichord* (1739) is mostly concerned with the highly specialised techniques of melodic ornamentation and thorough bass, while C. P. E. Bach's famous *Essay on the True Art of playing Keyboard Instruments* (1759), which also introduces the word 'taste' from time to time, does so in contexts which associate it with the decorative element in music, thus relating the word to our modern usage, as when we say, for instance, that a choice of clothes or the decoration of a room is in good or bad taste.

This latter meaning of the word links it with choice, and I believe it is mainly in this sense that Jane Austen intends it to be understood. Any aspect of music in which choice is allowable, whether it be tempo, dynamics, tone quality, or even (as with Geminiani and Bach), a matter of adding decorative elements or purely personal adaptations or amplifications of a given text, can therefore be described as taste. There might be rare occasions when Jane Austen also meant it to include what we vaguely call 'expression' (which really amounts to an ability to convey to the listener the performer's own emotional response to the music he is playing or singing), but I believe that an instinctive choice of the best among a variety of alternative possibilities is the true meaning of taste when it is used by Jane Austen in connection with music.

That Harriet Smith, in spite of Emma's tutelage, has still to learn that there are certain things a lady does not say is evident from her final comment on Jane Fairfax's playing:

> 'Besides, if she does play so very well, you know, it is no more than she is obliged to do, because she will have to teach. The Coxes were wondering last night if she would get into any great family.'
>
> (*Emma*, p. 232)

From this we may collect that Harriet feels herself in a position to look down on Jane Fairfax – that though she is herself no more than 'the natural daughter of somebody', she can, merely because of the liberal allowance made to her by her unknown father, feel superior to a young woman who is as far above her in intellect and accomplishments as she is by birth. It is obvious that Emma's patronage has done no more for Harriet than give her manners a little superficial polish. Harriet's natural intimates are the Miss Coxes rather than people like the elegant young mistress of Hartfield.

During the later part of the morning, most of the guests who had been at the Coles' party the night before assemble in Mrs Bates's sitting-room to see and hear the new pianoforte. By a clever piece of strategy, Frank manages to be alone with Jane for a few minutes, with only deaf old Mrs Bates (who is also temporarily blind because the rivet has come out of her spectacles) dozing by the fireside. The reader receives the impression that there has been some sort of emotional interchange between the lovers, and when Emma and Harriet arrive, summoned from a nearby shop by Miss Bates and Mrs Weston, they find Jane in a state of considerable nervous tension. She has to calm herself before she can begin to demonstrate the qualities of the pianoforte:

> At last Jane began, and though the first bars were feebly given, the powers of the instrument were gradually done full justice to. Mrs Weston had been delighted before, and was delighted again; Emma joined her in all her praise; and the pianoforté, with every proper discrimination, was pronounced to be altogether of the highest promise.
>
> (*Emma*, p. 241)

Frank now amuses himself by uttering a series of loaded remarks which Emma misinterprets, just as he intends her to, while Jane, whom he has appraised of Emma's suspicions, suffers in silence. She, of course, recognises that Frank's ambiguous words have hidden, but quite different, meanings for her, too. Smiling at Emma, Frank addresses Jane:

'Whoever Col. Campbell might employ, . . . the person
has not chosen ill. I heard a good deal of Col. Campbell's taste at Weymouth; and the softness of the
upper notes I am sure is exactly what he and *all that
party* would particularly prize. I dare say Miss Fairfax,
that he either gave his friend very minute directions, or
wrote to Broadwood himself. Do not you think so?'
Jane did not look round. She was not obliged to hear.

　　　　　　　　　　　　　　　　　　　(*Emma*, p. 241)

He carries on in the same strain, amusing Emma (and
himself) while teasing Jane. One cannot believe that he
realises how much distress he is causing his fiancée.
Frank is like a mischievous, spoiled boy; he has never been
taught to appreciate other people's feelings, but we,
who know how the story of *Emma* ends, must wonder how
much real happiness lies in store for Jane once she and
Frank are married. At last, apparently becoming a little
bored by his own double talk, he approaches Jane and
begs her to play something more:

'If you are very kind . . . it will be one of the waltzes we
danced last night; – let me live them over again. You
did not enjoy them as I did; you appeared tired the
whole time. I believe you were glad we danced no
longer; but I would have given worlds – all the worlds
one ever has to give – for another half hour.'

　　　　　　　　　　　　　　　　　　　(*Emma*, p. 242)

This speech, meant for Jane alone, illustrates Frank's
deviousness. He had not been able to dance with Jane the
night before. He had tried to encourage everyone to continue dancing so that he might, having done his duty by
Emma, claim Jane as his next partner, but Miss Bates
had been anxious to get home to her mother and the
dancing had ended too soon. He had then mendaciously
told Emma that he had been glad the dancing had ended
when it did – 'I must have asked Miss Fairfax, and her
languid dancing would not have agreed with me, after
yours.' Emma is still so satisfied by what she believes to
be her clever discovery of a secret romance between Jane

and Mr Dixon that though she overhears what Frank has said to Jane she fails to notice the discrepancy between his words of last night and what he says now. Frank's teasing of Jane is not very kind; he knows she must have wanted to dance with him as much as he with her; perhaps he also knows that she is beginning to take exception to his noticeable attentions to Emma, meant at first as a misleading stratagem, but fast becoming an agreeable diversion as well. The end of Frank's speech introduces an unexpected flash of irony – it is as if the authoress herself momentarily pushes him aside and directs our attention to the superficiality of his nothing-meaning platitude, 'I would have given worlds'.

Jane's answer to Frank's request is to play a waltz which he at once recognises as having a special significance for them both:

> 'What felicity it is to hear a tune again which *has* made one happy! – If I mistake not, that was danced at Weymouth.' (*Emma*, p. 242)

Jane rarely replies in words to Frank's dangerous, though excitingly cryptic talk; she hardly speaks throughout the whole scene, only answering him with her eyes and through her music. The waltz she had played was, of course, one they had danced together, perhaps on the very evening when their engagement had been formed. It probably had for them something like the symbolic meaning that Proust's celebrated *petite phrase* from the *Sonate de Vinteuil* had for Odette and Swann.

Jane now plays something else, and Frank, picking up some music from a chair, turns to Emma:

> 'Here is something quite new to me. Do you know it? – Cramer. – And here are a new set of Irish melodies . . . This was all sent with the instrument . . . I honour that part of the attention particularly: it shews it to have been thoroughly from the heart . . . True affection only could have prompted it.'
>
> Emma wished he would be less pointed.
> (*Emma*, p. 242)

She still thinks that Frank is speaking for her private amusement and that he is making thinly-veiled references to what she believes to be Jane's guilty secret. And so, of course, he is, though nothing he says means quite what Emma thinks it does. Jane, knowing the ideas that are in Emma's mind, is, naturally, very uncomfortable, but it is Emma who is the dupe. However, though she wishes he would be less pointed (and we are thankful that at last she begins to have qualms about his behaviour, which, taken at its face value, is both cruel and rather ill-bred), Emma happens to catch sight of a 'blush of consciousness' on Jane's cheek and the remains of a secret smile on her lips, and so feels 'less scruple in the amusement, and much less compunction with respect to her'. We must think that Emma's conscience has been too easily quieted.

Frank's mention of him reminds us that Cramer is the only composer named in all Jane Austen's novels. In 1814, John Baptist Cramer was already famous as a leading pianist and pianoforte teacher and also as a prolific composer. His works – concertos, chamber music, sonatas, variations and, above all, educational material, of which his celebrated 84 Studies are best remembered today – were no sooner written than they were printed, and they sold in vast quantities. His latest publications will have been prominently displayed in all of London's chief music shops and some of them would naturally have been included in Frank's selection of music for despatch with the instrument. As for the Irish melodies referred to – they were almost certainly the fourth set of Thomas Moore's immensely popular collections (the third collection, published in 1813, could scarcely have been considered as still quite new).

The *first* volume of *Moore's Irish Melodies* includes the tune which Jane now begins to play – a very old and celebrated air which is often called 'Robin Adair', though in Moore's collection it is given its original name, 'Eileen Aroon'. It is one of many ancient Celtic Songs which crossed the Irish Sea several times, sometimes changing nationality en route. Thought by many to be a Scottish air, it is, in fact, as genuinely Irish as Moore claimed it to be, and its nationality lends an added piquancy to Frank's whispered comment to Emma: 'She is playing Robin Adair at this moment – *his* favourite.' He intends Emma to understand from this that the old Irish air is the favourite of Mr Dixon, who, it should be remembered, is the owner of Baly-craig, a beautiful estate not far from Dublin. But it is highly likely that Frank is here speaking the literal truth, and that Jane is indeed playing *his* – that is, *Frank's* – favourite song. It would be a natural thing for her to do after playing 'their' waltz.

This superbly planned scene ends with the appearance of the novel's true hero, Mr Knightley. With supreme skill, the authoress allows everyone present to hear what he says (in characteristically resounding tones), but contrives that he should remain outside in the open air, untouched by the stifling atmosphere of intrigue and emotional tension which fills Mrs Bates's little sitting room. It is Miss Bates who, looking out of the window, sees Mr Knightley riding down the street. She runs into the adjoining room to open a casement and calls to him to put up his horse at the Crown Inn and join the admiring party round the new pianoforte. Mr Knightley, without dismounting, makes civil enquiries after them all, showing special concern for Jane's health, but he will not agree to enter the house. He is in a hurry and on his way to Kingston. Only when he hears that Emma is in the room does he waver – very well, he will come in for a few minutes. Miss Bates, chattering on, mentions that Mrs Weston and Mr Churchill are also there, whereupon Mr Knightley quickly changes his mind again – he cannot wait. Frank Churchill's presence has no attraction for *him* – quite the contrary, for the sight of Emma's laughing acceptance of Frank's attentions has become as odious to him as it is to Jane Fairfax.

Mr Knightley's integrity and strength of character and his outspoken way of talking, which is often laced with a dry wit peculiarly his own, are in striking contrast to the murmured double meanings and half-truths heard and over-heard against the background of Jane's pianoforte playing. While he speaks, though he remains invisible to all except Miss Bates, the party within must fall silent to listen, and in doing so it recedes, for the reader, into a kind of obscurity. When Mr Knightley goes on his way it is as if a strong, clear breeze had momentarily dispersed the clouds of 'hypocrisy and deceit' surrounding the unconscious Emma. She seems, indeed, to be aware that there has been a change. A spell has been broken – she becomes anxious to leave, and, rising quickly, with civil thanks and polite farewells, returns to Hartfield.

The Broadwood pianoforte has now almost served its main purpose. It has stimulated much lively discussion in Highbury and it has allowed many of the leading characters in *Emma* to reveal their thoughts and display their idiosyncrasies in conversation about its mysterious arrival. Dialogue, as a means of propulsion for the forwarding of her plots and for making her people rise from the page as if they were living realities, is a technical device which Jane Austen always uses with a mastery unsurpassed, and scarcely equalled, by any later writer. But though, after the tenth chapter of the second volume of *Emma* the pianoforte is no longer of importance as a talking point, music itself is used with great skill to portray the appalling conceit, vulgarity and affectation of a character who now makes her first appearance – Mrs Elton.

Mrs Elton is one of Jane Austen's finest creations: a woman who in real life would scarcely be bearable for even the regulation fifteen minutes of Emma's 'official' wedding visit to the vicarage, but about whom we can never read enough. Generations of 'Janeites' have delighted in Mrs Elton's pert assurance and her 'resolute stylishness', and not a few have taken a certain wicked pleasure in the outrages which she inflicts on Emma's dignity in the early stages of their acquaintance.

It is during the Eltons' return visit to Hartfield that

Emma herself, searching for a change of subject, hits on music:

> 'I do not ask whether you are musical, Mrs Elton. Upon
> these occasions, a lady's character generally precedes
> her; and Highbury has long known that you are a su-
> perior performer.'
>
> (*Emma*, pp. 276)

Mrs Elton's reply, replete with unnecessary emphases,
repetitions, mock-modesty and a general tone of smug
self-satisfaction, presents her with such an immediacy
that one wonders if Jane Austen can actually have met
her. It is a daunting thought. What Mrs Elton has to say
about music deserves extensive quotation:

> 'Oh! no, indeed; I must protest against any such idea.
> A superior performer! – very far from it, I assure you . . .
> I am dotingly fond of music – passionately fond; – and
> my friends say I am not entirely devoid of taste; but as
> to anything else, upon my honour my performance is
> *mediocre* to the last degree. You, Miss Woodhouse, I well
> know, play delightfully. I assure you it has been the
> greatest satisfaction, comfort and delight to me, to hear
> what a musical society I am got into. I absolutely
> cannot do without music. It is a necessary of life to me;
> and having always been used to a very musical society,
> both at Maple Grove and in Bath, it would have been a
> most serious sacrifice. I honestly said as much to Mr E.
> when he was speaking of my future home, and expressing
> his fears lest the retirement of it should be disagreeable
> . . . I honestly said that *the world* I could give up –
> parties, balls, plays – for I had no fear of retirement.
> Blessed with so many resources within myself, the world
> was not necessary to *me*. I could do very well without it.
> To those who had no resources it was a different thing;
> but my resources made me quite independent . . .
> "But", said I, "to be quite honest, I do not think I can
> live without something of a musical society. I condition
> for nothing else; but, without music, life would be a
> blank to me".'

Hardly waiting for Emma's slight reply, Mrs Elton, after hoping that they 'would have many sweet little concerts together', goes on to suggest that they should establish a musical club, with alternate weekly meetings at their respective houses:

> 'If *we* exert ourselves, I think we shall not be long in want of allies. Something of that nature would be particularly desirable for *me*, as an inducement to keep me in practice; for married women, you know – there is a sad story against them, in general. They are but too apt to give up music.'

There is an echo here of something we have heard before – something about married women who neglect their music once they have no further need for it (that is, once they are safely married). A moment's reflection reminds us whence the echo comes: it is from *Sense and Sensibility*, and it concerns Lady Middleton, whose songs, it will be recalled, 'brought into the family on her marriage . . . had lain ever since in the same position on the pianoforté.' Emma makes a token protest about Mrs Elton's evident determination to neglect her music, but secretly she is boiling with indignation at the lady's easy assumption of complete social equality between Hartfield and the vicarage:

> '. . . to propose that she and I should unite to form a musical club! One would fancy we were bosom friends!'
>
> (*Emma*, p. 279)

Poor Emma! One must smile a little at her injured dignity, but one can only concur with her final estimation of her visitor, as she politely says goodbye to both the Eltons at the close of their call at Hartfield: Mrs Elton is indeed 'a little upstart, vulgar being', and Emma speaks for every reader when she relieves her feelings with the exclamation 'Insufferable woman!'

One of Mrs Elton's numerous sins, in Emma's eyes, is her quick adoption of Jane Fairfax as a kind of protégée. Not long after the Eltons' visit to Hartfield, Emma has to listen to much gushing praise of Jane, who is evidently regarded by Mrs Elton as an inferior – a person whom she is honouring by her patronage, much as Emma feels herself to be honouring Harriet:

> 'Jane Fairfax is absolutely charming, Miss Woodhouse. – I quite rave about Jane Fairfax. – A sweet, interesting creature. So mild and ladylike – and with such talents! – I assure you I think she has very extraordinary talents. I do not scruple to say that she plays extremely well. I know enough of music to speak decidedly on that point. Oh! she is absolutely charming! You will laugh at my warmth – but upon my word, I talk of nothing but Jane Fairfax. – And her situation is so calculated to affect one! – Miss Woodhouse, we must exert ourselves and endeavour to do something for her. We must bring her forward. Such talents as hers must not be suffered to remain unknown.' (*Emma*, p. 282)

Knowing how Emma feels about Jane Fairfax, we can imagine her extreme irritation at being called upon (and by Mrs Elton, of all people) to assist in the launching of Jane into Highbury society – in itself an absurd proposal, since Jane was born in the town and has been known and admired there all her life. Mrs Elton goes on to outline her plans for her 'discovery':

> 'I shall certainly have her very often at my house, shall introduce her wherever I can, shall have musical parties to draw out her talents, and shall be constantly on the watch for an eligible situation. My acquaintance is so very extensive, that I have little doubt of hearing of something to suit her shortly.'
> (*Emma*, p. 284)

Mrs Elton's determination to find Jane an 'eligible situation' as a governess becomes a considerable trial to the object of her solicitude. Forced into unwelcome intimacy with the Eltons by poor Miss Bates's pathetically grateful acceptance of their frequent invitations, she has to exert herself to prevent Mrs Elton from making enquiries of all and sundry on her behalf:

'Thank you, but I would rather you did not mention the
subject . . . till the time draws nearer, I do not wish to
be giving any body trouble.'   (*Emma*, p. 300)

But Mrs Elton will not be deterred, and her insistence
eventually arouses in Jane an outburst of startling bitter-
ness against the profession for which she has been educated:

'There are places in town, offices, where inquiry would
soon produce something – Offices for the sale – not
quite of human flesh – but of human intellect.'

Mrs Elton appears to be slightly shocked: 'Oh! my dear,
human flesh!' But though Jane denies that she had, as
Mrs Elton supposed, intended a reference to the slave-
trade – 'governess-trade, I assure you, was all that I had
in view' – she adds, with painful intensity of feeling, that
the 'guilt' of those who trade in governesses and those who
trade in slaves may be widely different, 'but as to the
greater misery of the victims, I do not know where it lies.'
    It is strange that the same novel which contains this
stark exposition of the predicament of the single woman
without means who, because of social taboos, could earn
her living only by teaching, should have as a leading
character Mrs Weston, who, before her marriage, had
led a happy, reasonably secure and not too arduous life as
governess to Isabella and Emma Woodhouse. Jane
Fairfax's words make clear, however, that her creator
knew all about the indignities and privations endured by
such undowered spinsters as Miss Lee, the governess to the
Bertram girls at Mansfield Park. Jane Austen numbered
among her friends and acquaintances more than one such
unfortunate, and she must sometimes have reflected that
their unhappy lot might easily have been her own and
Cassandra's had it not been for the affectionate generosity
of their excellent brothers. [29] But it was to be left to her
successors, Charlotte and Anne Brontë, to use as a leading
theme the sad truth about the drudgery and contumely
which were too often the lot of the victims of the
'governess-trade'.

That Mrs Elton herself possesses something of the mentality of a slave marketeer is shown by her open assessment of Jane's musical abilities as purely financial assets. Too crude and vulgar to be aware of the indelicacy of what she is doing, she adds and subtracts until she reaches a satisfactory total of what she considers to be Jane's legitimate claims:

> '. . . with your superior talents, you have a right to move in the first circle. Your musical knowledge alone would entitle you to name your own terms, have as many rooms as you like, and mix in the family as much as you chose; – that is – I do not know – if you knew the harp, you might do all that, I am very sure; but you sing as well as play; – yes, I really believe you might, even without the harp, stipulate for what you chose . . .'
>
> (*Emma*, p. 301)

Truly, as Emma once exclaimed when sorely tried by Mrs Elton, 'there seems no limits to the licentiousness of that woman's tongue!'

Unfortunately for the readers of this book there *is* a limit, and it has been reached, for though Mrs Elton has a great deal to say in the third volume of *Emma*, none of it has to do with music. Those 'sweet little concerts' which she planned, if they ever took place, did so without the assistance of Miss Woodhouse, an alteration in Mrs Elton's manners towards her having brought to an end all civil exchanges between them. The only account we have (from Miss Bates) of an evening in the vicarage drawing-room contains no mention of music, though it is the fateful night when Jane, accidentally learning that Frank had left Highbury in a fit of pique after a lovers' quarrel, resolved at once to terminate their engagement and, with all the resolution of a voluntary sacrificial victim, to yield to Mrs Elton's insistence that she should accept a post as governess in the family of a certain Mrs Smallridge.

As for the Broadwood pianoforte, whose mysterious arrival monopolised the interest of Highbury society until the appearance on the scene of the newly-married Mrs

Elton gave it something else to talk about, it is not until after a further series of misunderstandings has 'promoted the general distress of the work', and when 'the tell-tale compression of the pages' as yet unread indicates that the novel is drawing towards its close that the instrument is mentioned again, and then not by Mrs Elton (whose speculations as to its provenance might have been worth hearing) but by Miss Bates.

Jane's emotional distress has made her ill, and Emma, herself much chastened by Mr Knightley's severe reprimand to her after her rudeness to Miss Bates at the famous picnic on Box Hill, calls on the Bateses to make her peace and to enquire after Jane. Jane will not see her, but Miss Bates, anxious and confused, makes her as welcome as she can and more than she deserves. Hearing of Jane's decision to go to Mrs Smallridge, Emma's glance strays to the silent pianoforte and Miss Bates observes it:

> 'Ay, I see what you are thinking of, the piano forté. What is to become of that? – Very true. Poor dear Jane was talking of it just now. – "You must go," said she. "You and I must part. You will have no business here. – Let it stay, however," said she; "give it house-room till Colonel Campbell comes back. I shall talk about it to him; he will settle for me; he will help me out of all my difficulties." – And to this day, I do believe, she knows not whether it was his present or his daughter's.'
>
> Now Emma was obliged to think of the piano-forté; and the remembrance of all her former fanciful and unfair conjectures was so little pleasing that she soon allowed herself to believe her visit had been long enough.
>
> (Emma, p. 384)

I have sometimes wondered why Emma, who does not, at this point in the story, know the truth about Jane and Frank, should suddenly decide that what Professor Liddell has called 'The Dixon Story' is unfair and fanciful. She is, of course, genuinely ashamed of herself after Mr Knightley's lecture, and all her better feelings are to the fore, but nothing has really happened to remove her misconceptions and suspicions about the reason for Jane's presence in Highbury or the giver of the pianoforte.

There remain two last references to the instrument to be mentioned. One occurs in the long letter of explanation and apology written by Frank Churchill to his step-mother, Mrs Weston, after his reconciliation with Jane Fairfax, an event made possible by the sudden, and apparently unregretted, death of Mrs Churchill, the aunt whose pride he feared to offend by admitting his intention to marry a penniless orphan:

> 'Of the pianoforté so much talked of, I feel it only necessary to say, that its being ordered was absolutely unknown to Miss F. – who would never have allowed me to send it, had any choice been given her.'
>
> (*Emma*, p. 439)

It is when Mr Knightley arrives at this passage during his reluctant perusal of Frank's letter (he only reads it to oblige Emma, for he would much prefer to talk about their recently formed engagement) that he exclaims:

> 'the pianoforte! Ah! That was the act of a very, very young man, one too young to consider whether the inconvenience of it might not very much exceed the pleasure. A boyish scheme, indeed!'
>
> (*Emma*, p. 446)

What Mr Knightley says is perfectly just, and, in view of the feelings of mistrust, jealousy and anger against Frank which had possessed him during most of their short acquaintance, he is remarkably forbearing about Frank's behaviour. But then, Mr Knightley can well afford to be in charity with all the world, for when he reads Frank's letter he and Emma have already come to understand one another, and with the declaration of their mutual love, have learned to know 'something so like perfect happiness that it could bear no other name.'

Admirers of *Emma*, however, cannot but be grateful that Frank's 'boyish scheme' was conceived and carried through, for without it the novel would have been a different, and perhaps a less entertaining work. The pianoforte's arrival in Highbury is an essential ingredient in the book's carefully structured plot, and certainly no more effective means could have been devised for arousing interest, speculation and discussion among a group of people living at close quarters in a small county town. And if, to our present way of thinking, the secrecy about Jane Fairfax's engagement to Frank Churchill seems absurd and unnecessary, it is the 'detective story' element introduced by that secret into the novel which intrigues everyone reading it for the first time, and which continues to interest and amuse even those whose frequent re-readings of it have given them an ever increasing delight in the technical brilliance and the subtlety of the characterisation displayed in this, the most perfect of Jane Austen's masterpieces.

CHAPTER IX

Persuasion

As *Persuasion* is a much shorter book than the two earlier Chawton novels there is less room in it for music. Yet it contains a scene which is unique in all Jane Austen's work – a scene in which an important, indeed a crucial movement of the story takes place during a public concert in the New Assembly Rooms at Bath, a venue familiar to the authoress from her early girlhood (though known to her as the Upper Rooms), and where, as we have seen, she attended concerts during the years of her residence in that city. It is the only time that Jane Austen allows us a brief glimpse of the professional concert world of her day, all her other uses for music being limited to its various domestic forms.

Anne Elliot, the elegant and charming heroine of *Persuasion*, is a good amateur pianist – certainly a better player than Emma Woodhouse, though probably not in the same class as Jane Fairfax. But Anne receives none of the plaudits and gratitude which invariably follow the performances of those young ladies, for she is essentially a Cinderella figure (in this, though in little else, she is like Fanny Price), even to the extent of being provided with a pair of sisters who, if not physically ugly, are certainly very deficient in that beauty of character which Anne possesses in such large measure.

When we first meet Anne we find her living in an almost entirely alien environment with only one true friend, Lady Russell, to love her and value her as she should be valued. Lady Russell is a good woman, but she has her limitations: her manners are always a little too formal and she seems somewhat lacking in imagination. There is evidence that she also lacks any taste for music, even music performed by her beloved Anne. In this respect Anne was worse off than Marianne Dashwood, for though Elinor may not always have listened to Marianne's playing in a suitably religious silence, she admired and fully appreciated her sister's abilities, whereas Anne's playing was for herself alone:

> She knew when she played she was giving pleasure only to herself; but this was no new sensation: excepting one short period of her life, she had never, since the age of fourteen, never since the loss of her dear mother, known the happiness of being listened to, or encouraged by any just appreciation or real taste. In music she had been always used to feel alone in the world.
>
> *(Persuasion*, p. 47)

The short period in her life alluded to, the period when she *had* been listened to with appreciation, had occurred during her nineteenth year, when she and a certain dashing young naval officer had fallen in love and formed an engagement which had at once met with crushing dis- approval from her father, the pompous, conceited baronet, Sir Walter Elliot, and her elder sister, Elizabeth. Even Lady Russell thought it imprudent and premature, and used her influence to persuade Anne to dissolve it. At nineteen, Anne's nature was too pliable to withstand opposition from such a source. She might have learned to do without her family's sanction, but Lady Russell's disapprobation of her engagement was another matter. On her opinion she was accustomed to rely, and now it prevailed over Anne's own desires. She yielded to persua- sion, and the dissolution of her engagement to Commander Wentworth had been followed by eight years of sorrow, regret and dwindling hope until, at the age of twenty- seven, when the story begins, Anne's looks, too, had begun to fade.

The first hint we receive that Anne is musical occurs during a conversation with her younger sister, Mary, who is the wife of Charles Musgrove, heir to the estate of Uppercross. Sir Walter Elliot, as a consequence of much extravagance and mismanagement, has been forced to let his mansion, Kellynch Hall, and has taken a house in Bath, where he and his eldest daughter can lead an existence of snobbish exclusiveness and 'heartless elegance' at relatively little expense. Anne, however, has not yet joined them there: she is beginning a long visit to Mary and Charles at Uppercross Cottage, which is within walking distance of the Great House, the home of Charles's parents and their large family, of which the two eldest daughters, Louisa and Henrietta, both have parts to play in the events which will later bring about the happy ending which is traditional in every Cinderella story. Anne has been trying to tell Mary (who is not particularly interested) of the various duties which have fallen to her lot in connection with the move to Bath, and she mentions that she has had 'books and music to divide'.

By one of those coincidences which are not as frequent in real life as in fiction, Sir Walter's tenant at Kellynch, Admiral Croft, is the brother-in-law of Anne's former lover, Commander Wentworth, now raised to the rank of captain. Naturally, Captain Wentworth may be expected to visit his sister, Mrs Croft, and as Kellynch is only a few miles from Uppercross calls of ceremony must be made; the Crofts and Captain Wentworth must return them; and so, in the natural course of events, Anne and Frederick Wentworth find themselves, once more, in the same room.

It is a trying situation for them both. Anne, still in love with the handsome Frederick, suffers deeply and can scarcely speak. The latter, smarting from the wound his heart had received eight years previously, is cold and distant to Anne but all brilliance, vitality and good humour to everyone else – particularly to the two Miss Musgroves.

Much of the action of this part of the story takes place

in the old-fashioned square parlour of the Great House,

> . . . to which the present daughters of the house were
> gradually giving the proper air of confusion by a grand
> piano forte and a harp, flower-stands and little tables
> placed in every direction.   (*Persuasion*, p. 40)

In this room the guests assemble after the dinner parties
which are frequently given by the hospitable Musgroves,
and there, on numerous occasions, the evening ends with
an impromptu ball.

Anne, quiet and reserved, and, of course, several years
senior to the Miss Musgroves, is not really expected to
join in the fun. When the idea of dancing is put forward,
she invariably seats herself at the pianoforte and 'plays
country dances to them by the hour together.'

Old Mr and Mrs Musgrove, wealthy, comfortably built
and kind-hearted, are fond of Anne, and they often wish
it were she, and not Mary, who had married their eldest
son; but being quite without discrimination in musical
matters, they value Anne's playing only for its usefulness
in promoting the pleasures of their children:

> She played a great deal better than either of the Miss
> Musgroves; but having no voice, no knowledge of the
> harp, and no fond parents to sit by and fancy them-
> selves delighted, her performances were very little
> thought of, only out of civility, or to refresh the others . . .
> Mr and Mrs Musgrove's fond partiality for their own
> daughters' performance, and total indifference to any
> other person's, gave her more pleasure for their sakes
> than mortification for her own.   (*Persuasion*, pp. 46–7)

Nothing recommends Anne's musical powers to Mr and
Mrs Musgrove more than her willingness to 'act as musician' when dancing is proposed, and it is her readiness to
oblige in this way which often draws from them some such
words of faint praise as –

> 'Well done, Miss Anne! very well done indeed! Lord
> bless me! how those little fingers of yours fly about!'
> (*Persuasion*, p. 47)

Beautiful and moving though it is (it is my own
favourite among Jane Austen's novels), *Persuasion* is not a
completely finished work. It would certainly have been
revised had Jane Austen lived long enough to prepare it
for the press, and perhaps one of the signs of its slight
inequality is the fact that it abounds in coincidences.
Among these is the story of Dick Musgrove, a younger
brother of Charles who, having proved 'stupid and un-
manageable' at home, had been shipped off to sea as a
'middy', only to die, most conveniently for his relatives,
in some far-off foreign clime a year or so later. Needless
to say, one of the ships, though not the last, in which
Dick had 'served' had been commanded by Captain
Wentworth.

Jane Austen has been adversely criticised for what
some people consider to be her rather heartless account of
Mrs Musgrove's 'large, fat sighings' over the fate of the
unloved and almost forgotten son of whom she is reminded
when she realises that it is Captain Wentworth, newly
come among them, who had been kind to Dick while the
boy had been on his ship. It might be as well for such
critics to remember that Mrs Musgrove did not exist outside Jane Austen's imagination. For my part, I have always
been much more struck by the ease and ruthlessness with
which a delinquent could be quietly disposed of in
Regency England. No psychiatric treatment or 'special'
schools for Dick Musgrove: if it was not quite a case of his
being 'sent to the galleys', it was certainly a matter of
submitting him to the strictest of disciplines under the
harshest of conditions – life on a man-of-war. And he did
not survive it.

It is on the evening of the day when Mr and Mrs
Musgrove have been looking through the few letters they
had ever received from Dick in order to confirm that he
really was, for a time, on Captain Wentworth's ship, that
the family from the Great House is invited to spend the
evening at Uppercross Cottage. Anne and Mary are
listening for the sound of the carriage (it is a rainy evening)

when Henrietta arrives on foot to explain that because her parents are feeling depressed she has walked on in advance to make room in the carriage for the harp:

> '. . . papa and mamma are out of spirits this evening, especially mamma; she is thinking so much of poor Richard! And we agreed it would be best to have the harp, for it seems to amuse her more than the piano-forte . . .'   (*Persuasion*, p. 50)

It is a new idea to us that the harp can be regarded as an 'amusing' instrument, but, after all, was it not Rameau who defined music as an art which should aim, above all, to please and to 'divert'? Mrs Musgrove, as a child of the eighteenth century (and an unmusical one at that) can perhaps be forgiven for failing to take the harp *au sérieux*.

One interesting fact emerges from this episode: the Musgroves would hardly have gone to the length of moving their own grand pianoforte down to Uppercross Cottage for an evening, so it may be understood that there was already, perhaps not a grand, but certainly a square pianoforte installed there; from which it follows that Mary had also been taught something of pianoforte playing, though, like other young married women – Lady Middleton, Mrs Elton – she had probably neglected her music since her marriage. When we continue this line of thought, it at once strikes us that if her two younger sisters had been taught to play it is next to impossible that Elizabeth Elliot should be quite without musical accomplishments. One cannot suppose that Miss Elliot's playing (and, perhaps, singing) will have given much pleasure to discerning listeners. She may have acquired a certain amount of 'execution', but it is unlikely that such a hard, unfeeling personality as hers would have possessed any of the natural 'taste' which was, without doubt, a noticeable feature of Anne's playing.

We do not know which of the Miss Musgroves played the harp. Perhaps they both played it. Certainly they both

played the pianoforte (we have already been told that
their pianoforte playing was much inferior to Anne's),
and it will be remembered that Fanny Knight, Jane
Austen's niece, played both instruments. Whether they
played duets for harp and pianoforte must also be conjecture, though it is likely that they did. After all, 'Lessons'
for harp and pianoforte were played at Mrs Henry
Austen's party, in 1811, such duets having been widely
popular since the virtuoso performances of the great pianist, J. L. Dussek, and his harpist wife, Sophia Dussek,
née Corri, who were working together in London from
1792 to 1802. Dussek wrote a number of sonatas for harp
and pianoforte, and many lesser composers followed his
example. But even in extremely capable hands, the sound
of this combination of instruments can be disagreeable to
sensitive ears, while performances by amateurs like the
Miss Musgroves would be likely to set the teeth on edge.
However, Mrs Musgrove apparently found it 'amusing'
(or at least the harp parts), though I suspect that she was
really more distracted from her sorrows by the visual
interest of harp-playing than by the music itself.

Mrs Musgrove's restrospective sorrowings over the loss
of the son who 'had been very little cared for at any time
by his family, though quite as much as he deserved'
occurred before Captain Wentworth had actually joined
his relations at Kellynch. Once the Crofts had introduced
their brother to the Musgroves, however, the acquaintance
quickly became friendship, and Captain Wentworth took
to riding over to Uppercross most mornings of the week.
This soon gave rise to ideas among the onlookers, including the little party at the Cottage, that he might have
intentions towards one or other of the Miss Musgroves.
Charles gave it for Louisa; Mary for Henrietta. Anne
wondered, doubted, remembered and at last concluded
that though Captain Wentworth might not at present be
in love with either of the young ladies there was no knowing what might happen in the future. He certainly aroused
in both girls an ecstasy of admiration which they displayed

without reserve on the increasingly numerous occasions
when the Kellynch family joined their new friends in the
'old-fashioned square parlour' of the Great House at
Uppercross. At these parties Captain Wentworth rarely
spoke to Anne, and when he was obliged to do so it was
always with distant politeness. Evidently the past was not
to be forgotten or forgiven. He was, of course, unaware
of her feelings, and did not consider that his deliberate
avoidance of her might be inflicting a painful wound.

The reader suffers with Anne during those convivial
evenings at Uppercross. She had to watch her former
fiancé basking in the admiration of a whole bevy of starry-
eyed females (the Musgroves' cousins, the Miss Hayters,
were also 'admitted to the honour of being in love with
him'); his tales of stirring events at sea were listened to
with rapt attention and punctuated by flattering gasps
of wonder and excitement, while the effect of his personal
attractions on Louisa and Henrietta was obvious for all
to see. Naturally enough, it was primarily for them that
his brilliance and charm were displayed, though his innate good manners also enabled him to attend, with suitably sympathetic gravity, to Mrs Musgrove's mournings
over the fate of the defunct but unregretted Dick.

Anne knew that her own delicate beauty had faded,
perhaps for ever, and she was soon made aware that Captain Wentworth had noticed the change in her, for Mary,
with an insensibility which seems to us very unkind
(though she knew nothing of their former engagement)
but which was perhaps merely sisterly, reported Frederick
as having said of Anne that she was so altered he should
scarcely have known her. It is not surprising that Anne's
spirits were depressed:

> The evening ended with dancing. On its being pro-
> posed, Anne offered her services, as usual, and though
> her eyes would sometimes fill with tears as she sat at the
> instrument, she was extremely glad to be employed,
> and desired nothing in return but to be unobserved.
> *(Persuasion*, p. 71)

Anne does not, however, remain entirely unobserved by Frederick. He may avoid addressing her directly, but he is, nevertheless, aware of her as she sits at the pianoforte, 'her fingers mechanically at work, proceeding for half an hour together, equally without error and without conscious-ness.' With the extreme sensitivity born of love, Anne *feels* Frederick watching her while she plays. She imagines that he may, perhaps, be 'trying to trace the ruins of the face that had once charmed him', and once she becomes aware that he must have spoken of her:

> . . . she was sure of his having asked his partner whether Miss Elliot never danced? The answer was, 'Oh! no, never; she has quite given up dancing. She had rather play. She is never tired of playing.' Once, too, he spoke to her. She had left the instrument on the dancing being over, and he had sat down to try to make out an air which he wished to give the Miss Musgroves an idea of. Unintentionally she returned to that part of the room; he saw her, and, instantly rising, said with studied politeness,
> 'I beg your pardon, Madam, this is your seat;' and though she immediately drew back with a decided negative, he was not to be induced to sit down again.
> Anne did not wish for more of such looks and speeches. His cold politeness, his ceremonious grace, were worse than anything.
>
> (*Persuasion*, p. 72)

Despite the authoress's assurance that Anne had drifted unintentionally towards the group clustered round the pianoforte, there is something very like a 'Freudian slip' about her action. It might well be the last thing she con-sciously wished to do, but the subconscious can play unkind tricks on those who are in love, and that Anne should move instinctively towards Frederick need surprise no one who understands anything of the psychology of lovers. What *is* faintly surprising, is that Frederick should know enough about the pianoforte keyboard even to attempt to 'make out an air' for the benefit of the Miss

Musgroves. As we have seen, some of Jane Austen's young men, among them John Willoughby and Frank Churchill, do possess a certain amount of musical knowledge which goes well enough with their personalities, but gallant Captain Wentworth belongs to a different category: he is essentially a glamour hero – a man of action who would have neither the time nor the opportunity in his life at sea to cultivate the arts. That he might have possessed quite as much instinctive artistic 'taste' as any other character in Jane Austen's novels we can believe (it was he, after all, who had once been Anne's only appreciative listener), but he seems out of place when actually seated at the keyboard.

Among the most important and dramatic scenes in *Persuasion* are those which take place at Lyme. The future movement of the plot hinges on events which occur there during what begins as a brief pleasure excursion but ends in near-tragedy. Louisa Musgrove's fall on the Cobb (a stone promontory projecting into the sea) precipitates an immediate crisis in Frederick's life, for it shocks him into the realisation that though he does not love her he is in honour bound to ask her to marry him should she recover. Louisa's own future is also materially affected by her accident – it eventually brings about her marriage to another man.

At Lyme, too, the cast of *Persuasion* is considerably enlarged. There we meet certain characters who have been, until now, mere names – the Harvilles, Captain Benwicke, and Anne's cousin, Mr Elliot. The cousins have never met, and Anne is unaware of her relationship to the gentleman, a fellow guest at the inn (another coincidence), who is so obviously struck by her beauty (temporarily revived, it appears, by Lyme's fresh sea breezes) that Captain Wentworth's attention is drawn to her anew. It is from this moment that his love for her, which had been latent but never dead, begins to revive. Louisa's accident then shows Frederick the superiority of Anne's character – her competence and cool-headedness during the panic which follows Louisa's fall (the two other young women

of the party faint and have hysterics, and even Captain
Wentworth, like the other men, seems astonishingly
helpless in the emergency) – and it proves to be the real
turning-point in their long-interrupted love affair, though
much else will happen before they are finally united in
perfect happiness.

Music, of course, can play no part in these scenes, most
of which take place in the open air, and we must follow
Anne's progress back to Uppercross, and, after a very short
stay with Lady Russell at Kellynch Lodge, to her arrival
in Bath before the subject recurs. It is on the very first
evening after she has rejoined her father and elder sister
in their new house in Camden Place[30] that she is presented
to Mr Elliot, who learns with astonishment and pleasure
that the object of his admiration at Lyme had been his own
first cousin.

From this moment Anne and Mr Elliot are thrown very
much together, and it soon becomes apparent, at least to
Lady Russell and to Mr Elliot's own circle, that he will,
in the course of time (he is a recent widower), ask Anne to
marry him. Lady Russell believes that it will be an
eminently suitable match, but Anne, though she quite
enjoys her cousin's company, remains constant to her
first love. At twenty-seven she can rely on her own judgment and she is no longer vulnerable to Lady Russell's
attempts at persuasion. Should Mr Elliot ever make Anne
a proposal she intends to refuse him.

Jane Austen now performs a brilliantly successful
manoeuvre: she assembles almost all the remaining characters of *Persuasion* in Bath, and she does so with a natural-
ness and an apparent ease which conceal the most
consummate art. The Musgroves (with the exception of
Louisa, not yet recovered enough to travel), Captain and
Mrs Harville, Mary and Charles, Admiral and Mrs Croft,
all arrive in Bath, and in each case there is a perfectly valid
reason for their coming. Perhaps the Admiral's gouty
foot may seem a little contrived, but, after all, why should
he *not* have a gouty foot? It was a common enough com-

plaint at his time of life, and the waters of Bath were an
equally common panacea for it. It is, of course, essential
that the Crofts should be in Bath so that Frederick, now
freed from all moral obligations to Louisa Musgrove by her
engagement to Captain Benwicke, may join them there.

Frederick's first meeting with Anne takes place in
Molland's shop, in Milsom Street.[31] It does not present
him in quite so dashing a light as usual: it is true that we
would not expect him to be wearing his officer's sword in
peace time, but that much less heroic accoutrement, an
umbrella, prudently purchased against Bath's winter
rains and now hooked over his arm, seems oddly out of
character. It is a wet day, however, and his umbrella
provides him with an excuse to offer its protection and the
support of his arm to Anne during her walk back to
Camden Place. But he has been forestalled, and he has the
mortification of seeing her move away, squired by her
cousin, while he overhears the gossiping speculations of the
other customers in Molland's ('Mr Elliot does not dislike
his cousin, I fancy?' 'Oh! no, that is clear enough. One
can guess what will happen there.)'. It is evident that the
Bath social world of 1815 must have been extremely small.

The stage is now prepared for the great series of scenes
which bring this beautiful, if very slightly imperfect,
book to its admirable concluding chapters – to the
wonderfully moving account of Anne's conversation with
Captain Harville during her visit to the Musgroves
at the White Hart Inn, and Captain Wentworth's famous
love letter, renewing his proposal of marriage, written in
Anne's actual presence. This scene, Jane Austen's
inspired 'second thought', replaces an earlier, less emo-
tionally highly-charged ending to the story, and it is
preceded by another celebrated 'set piece' – the concert at
the New Assembly Rooms during which Mr Elliot's
attentions to Anne seem to confirm Frederick's fears of an
impending engagement between the cousins. The reader
shares Anne's confused emotions – pleasure, anxiety,
triumph – when she realises that, Cinderella though she

may be to her own family, her Prince Charming is now extremely jealous of his supposed rival.

Visitors to present-day Bath can see the great concert room at the New Assembly Rooms – not, to be sure, the building known to Jane Austen (that, alas! was gutted by fire during the air raids of 1942) but an exact replica of it, faithful to the smallest detail, which was opened to the public in 1963; they may also see the famous octagon room in which the Elliots' party was joined by the Dowager Viscountess Dalrymple, her daughter, the Honourable Miss Carteret, and other, less exalted members of their exclusive circle, before proceeding 'with all the consequence in their power' into the concert room.

At this point one turns to the files of the *Bath Chronicle* (which had proved so informative about the music heard in Bath by Jane Austen herself and even about that which could have been enjoyed by Catherine Morland in 1798) for details of the programme which, according to Dr Chapman's reckoning, must have taken place on a Wednesday late in February, 1815. The Wednesdays of that month fell on the 1st, 8th, 15th and 22nd. February 22nd was, therefore, almost certainly the date of the concert which played such an important part in the romance of Anne Elliot and Frederick Wentworth, and, sure enough, the *Bath Chronicle* confirms that a concert in the New Assembly Rooms was given on that date. The *Chronicle*'s advertisement of it, however, is disappointingly brief, giving little more than the names of some of the principal performers. Fortunately a rival Bath newspaper – the *Bath Journal* – carried a much more detailed list of the varied musical delights prepared for the 'Nobility, Gentry and his friends in general' by the concert's organiser, a Mr A. Loder.

Here it must be mentioned that, with the death of Vincenzo Rauzzini, in 1810, the management of the winter Subscription Concerts in Bath had been taken over by an Irishman, a virtuoso flautist named Andrew Ashe, who had previously worked in Brussels, London and Dublin, and that though something of the *cachet* given to the city's musical life by the internationally renowned Rauzzini had inevitably been lost, Mr Ashe had succeeded in organising very creditable musical seasons between 1810 and 1817. He usually managed to engage some star performers to add lustre to his programmes, and early in 1814 the greatest Italian soprano of the day, Angelica Catalani, had made several appearances at Ashe's concerts and aroused immense excitement and enthusiasm, while during the same season such famous instrumentalists as the pianist, Ferdinand Ries (Beethoven's pupil) and the violinist, Madame Gautherot, had also been warmly acclaimed.

The 1814–15 season of the Subscription Concerts came to an end on February 15th with the ninth concert of the series. The concert of February 22nd, therefore, was an addition to the normal winter musical season: it was, in fact, a business speculation by a member of a well-known family of Bath musicians, the Loders, who owned successful music shops at 46 Milson Street and 4 Orange Grove. Mr Loder was unable to call upon the services of such 'stars' (among them the celebrated pianist, Kalkbrenner, and several Italian opera singers) as those who had graced Ashe's season, but he was very well supported by numerous local colleagues. As many as nine solo singers took part in the concert and among them was Mrs Ashe, the wife of Rauzzini's successor. We have met Mrs Ashe before: she was none other than 'Bath's own little Syren', that very Miss Comer whose sweet, plaintive tones had delighted Catherine Morland long ago in 1798. Miss Comer, who had been one of Rauzzini's best pupils, had married in 1799, the year after Catherine's visit to Bath, and, as Mrs Ashe, had since become a mainstay of the city's musical life, no important concert being considered complete without her. On this occasion, too, a *Mr* Comer, evidently a relative of Mrs Ashe, made his first appearance as a singer at the Assembly Rooms.

The first 'Act' of the concert began with a 'Grand Sinfonia' (composer unnamed) and continued with a glee for four mens' voices. There followed a duet and a solo song, after which a Mr Percival performed a violoncello concerto of his own composition. Mrs Ashe then made her first appearance. She was succeeded by Mr T. Cooke,[32] and the 'Act' ended with an Italian *Terzetto*, '*Cheve par*', sung by Mrs Ashe, Mr A. Loder and Mr Comer. It was probably the text of 'Cheve par' which Anne so obligingly translated for Mr Elliot during the subsequent interval.

The second 'Act' of the concert, after an introductory Overture, continued with a selection of glees, solo songs and duets. Then came the evening's *pièce de résistance* – Beethoven's 'Grand Fantasia for Piano Forte solo with an accompaniment for full band and chorus'. One must admire the enterprise of the musicians of Bath in performing this very novel work. It is a rarity even today, and in 1815 it must have been considered decidedly 'modern'. The solo pianoforte part was played by a local infant prodigy, Master Henry Field, son of Thomas Field, the organist of Bath Abbey.[33] Little Henry's father had himself been something of a prodigy and had appeared as a pianoforte soloist at Rauzzini's concerts, but on this occasion the proud father was content merely to play the drums in the orchestra while his brilliant son drew the applause of the connoisseurs.[34] After the Beethoven Fantasia, Braham's popular ballad, 'The Death of Abercrombie' sung by Mr Cooke, must have made a curiously bathetic impression; but the concert promoter had to consider all his patrons: the 'highbrows' had been well catered for and now it was the turn of those with more 'popular' tastes. Glees, solo songs and an Italian *Quartetto* brought the vocal part of the evening to an end, and the customary 'full piece' for the orchestra, which rounded off the very long programme, was probably given somewhat perfunctory attention.

Among the members of the orchestra that night was one of particular interest: leading the orchestral 'cellos was Alexander Herschel, younger brother of the great astronomer, William Herschel. Both the Herschel brothers

were brilliant musicians (William had been, for a time,
Rauzzini's predecessor as director of the Bath Subscription
Concerts) and they also shared a like passion for scientific
subjects, particularly astronomy. Alexander had acted as
his brother's assistant in many of their earlier scientific
experiments, but the paths of their lives had diverged when
William's growing fame as an astronomer led, after his
discovery of the planet, Uranus, to his appointment as
astronomer royal and to his abandonment of professional
music-making as a career. William left Bath, but
Alexander remained there, and for many years he was a
prominent figure in the musical life of Somerset. Catherine,
the Herschel brothers' devoted sister, wrote in her remi-
niscences, 'The solos of my brother Alexander on the
violoncello were exquisite.' Alexander Herschel's partici-
pation in Loder's benefit concert must have been one of his
last appearances in the city. Shortly afterwards, an injury
to his knee incapacitated him, and in September, 1816,
he returned to his native Hanover where he remained
until his death five years later.[35] To the older generations
of Bath's music-lovers Alexander Herschel was a familiar
and much-admired part of their musical pleasures, but the
Elliots, as relative newcomers, will have been unaware
of his eminence in his profession and of his close connection with the famous astronomer. In any case, Anne, and
perhaps her cousin, would have been the only members of
the party to be genuinely interested.

We now know a great deal about the music with which
Anne was fully prepared to be delighted on that Wednesday evening in February, 1815. She was in no mood to
find fault with anything she heard. Having enjoyed a most
satisfactory conversation with Captain Wentworth in the
octagon room immediately before the concert began, she
was in a glow of happiness and ready to be pleased by
everything:

> Anne's mind was in a most favourable state for the
> entertainment of the evening: it was just occupation
> enough: she had feelings for the tender, spirits for the

gay, attention for the scientific, and patience for the
wearisome; and had never liked a concert better, at
least during the first act. Towards the close of it, in the
interval succeeding an Italian song, she explained the
words of the song to Mr Elliot. – They had a concert
bill between them.

(Persuasion, p. 186)

A few of the actual concert bills (we should call them
programmes) of concerts in Regency Bath have been
preserved. They do not contain the explanatory or descrip-
tive notes to which we are nowadays accustomed, but they
invariably print the texts of the vocal music in full. The
majority of these are in Italian.

It is easy to visualise the scene as Frederick saw it, with
Anne's head and her cousin's inclined towards one
another so that they might study together the words printed in the concert bill. Anne was merely engaged in
giving Mr Elliot a rough translation of the Italian text of
the song they had just heard (her general culture, like her
creator's, was evidently considerable, for not only was she
well-read in her own language but she had a working
knowledge of French and Italian as well), but the impression an onlooker might receive would be of an attractive
young couple deep in intimate converse. Mr Elliot, with
his compliments and hints, did in fact begin to adopt a
discreetly flirtatious manner, but Anne, preoccupied with
her thoughts of Frederick, scarcely noticed it and hardly
had time to laugh his words aside before the gentleman's
attention was claimed by the other ladies of the party.

The first 'Act' of the concert now being over, Anne
hoped that Frederick would make good use of the opportunity to talk to her again, and so remained in her seat
during the interval while the others went in search of tea.

He did not come however. Anne sometimes fancied she
discerned him at a distance, but he never came. The
anxious interval wore away unproductively. The others
returned, the room filled again, benches were reclaimed
and re-possessed, and another hour of pleasure or of

penance was to be set out, another hour of music was to
give delight or the gapes, as real or affected taste for it
prevailed. To Anne, it chiefly wore the prospect of an
hour of agitation. She could not quit that room in peace
without seeing Captain Wentworth once more, without
the interchange of one friendly look.

(Persuasion, p. 189)

In re-seating themselves, the members of the Elliots'
party now change places, and Anne, 'by some removals
and a little scheming of her own', manages to establish
herself near the end of the bench and within reach of
passers-by. Her stratagem works in part – Captain Wentworth approaches, but he seems depressed and hesitant
and

> . . . only by very slow degrees came at last near enough
> to speak to her . . . He began by speaking of the concert,
> gravely . . . owned himself disappointed, had expected
> better singing; and, in short, must confess that he should
> not be sorry when it was over. Anne replied, and spoke
> in defence of the performance so well, and yet in allow-
> ance for his feelings, so pleasantly, that his countenance
> improved, and he replied again with almost a smile.
> They talked for a few minutes more; the improvement
> held; he even looked down towards the bench, as if he
> saw a place on it well worth occupying; when, at that
> moment, a touch on her shoulder obliged Anne to turn
> round. – It came from Mr Elliot. He begged her par-
> don, but she must be applied to, to explain Italian
> again . . . Anne could not refuse; but never had she
> sacrificed to politeness with a more suffering spirit . . .
> when she was her own mistress again . . . she found her-
> self accosted by Captain Wentworth, in a reserved yet
> hurried sort of farewell. 'He must wish her goodnight.
> He was going – he should get home as fast as he could.'
> 'Is not this song worth staying for?' said Anne,
> suddenly struck by an idea which made her yet more
> anxious to be encouraging.
> 'No!' he replied impressively, 'there is nothing worth
> my staying for;' and he was gone directly.

(Persuasion, p. 190)

Captain Wentworth may well have been genuinely disappointed by the evening's singing, for Mr Loder and his friends, even including the popular Mrs Ashe, cannot have quite equalled the standard set by the celebrated Madame Sessi and the Signori Marzochi and Quarrantotti, leading singers from the King's Theatre in London, who had drawn the crowds to Mr Ashe's Subscription Concerts earlier in February. We know that Frederick Wentworth could discriminate in musical matters. Nevertheless, his words to Anne clearly have a double meaning which he fully intends her to understand. For Frederick is by now wildly jealous of Mr Elliot and Anne sees it with a thrill of pleasure ('the gratification was exquisite'), though her second thoughts are rather less happy, for she realises the difficulty of finding a means to correct his mistaken suspicions. But we need no longer be concerned about her future happiness, for we know that the lovers will come to understand one another, and that 'perfect felicity' cannot be long delayed. We might, however, before leaving the concert room, give a thought to the curious concert manners of the time; for all those final exchanges between Anne, her cousin and Captain Wentworth took place after the second 'Act' had begun. We do not know which overture was providing the background music for their conversation, but they paid it such scant attention that they cannot have known much about it themselves. At least we may be thankful that their little drama was not played out under the very noses of the long-suffering musicians, for the Elliots' party, we are told, did not occupy 'the seats of grandeur' round the orchestra, as might have been expected. Lady Dalrymple, whose wishes were, of course, always deferred to, chose 'to be farther off'.

Had Jane Austen kept to her original plan for the completion of *Persuasion* we should have had some further references to the concert in a very finely-written scene of general explanation and *éclaircissement*, set in Admiral Croft's Bath lodgings, during which Frederick. having realised his error about Anne's feelings for her cousin, declares his love for her and renews his offer of marriage.[36] But who could possibly regret the authoress's decision to jettison the whole of that scene in favour of the intricately designed and triumphantly successful penultimate chapter of her final version – that marvellous composition which she never surpassed elsewhere?

As a creator of character Jane Austen has sometimes been compared to Shakespeare – notably by Lord Macaulay and, more recently, by Mr J. B. Priestley.[37] This is not the place to embark on a discussion of the appropriateness, or otherwise, of such a literary comparison. Instead, I would suggest that this great artist's work at its best can only be likened to some of music's finest achievements, and that for anything comparable to the dénouement of *Persuasion* one must turn to Mozart – to the music of the sublime final act of *The Magic Flute*, for instance: a great masterpiece which, like Jane Austen's finest pages, combines simplicity and beauty of detail with absolute clarity of form and with the expression of deeply felt, but perfectly controlled emotion.

CHAPTER X

Jane Austen's Music Books: The Chawton Collection

THE COLLECTION of music books consisting of volumes which were either owned by or well known to Jane Austen is at present divided into two parts. The more important, since it includes much manuscript music in her own hand, is housed in the Jane Austen Museum at Chawton. It will be called here the Chawton Collection. The other, which is at present in the care of descendants of James Austen, Jane's eldest brother, will be called the Second Collection. It does not appear to contain any authentic Jane Austen manuscripts but it is nevertheless of great interest because it includes items which are relevant to the musical references in both *Mansfield Park* and *Emma*. The two collections will be separately discussed.

In a letter written by Jane Austen on November 17th, 1798, we come upon this significant phrase: 'an artist cannot do anything slovenly'. The writer was not referring to her own genius; she was merely making a joke about a carefully-finished little drawing which she had enclosed for the amusement of her nephew, George. Nevertheless, she was stating what was, in her view, an important truth: that an artist worth his salt is always careful over detail. Jane Austen, herself a supremely great artist, was unlikely to produce slovenly work of any kind, least of all work involving the use of her pen, and this is nowhere more evident than in her volumes of exquisitely-copied manuscript music. They are, in their way, as clearly and elegantly written as the tragically few extant manuscripts of her mature literary works.

ILLUSTRATIONS

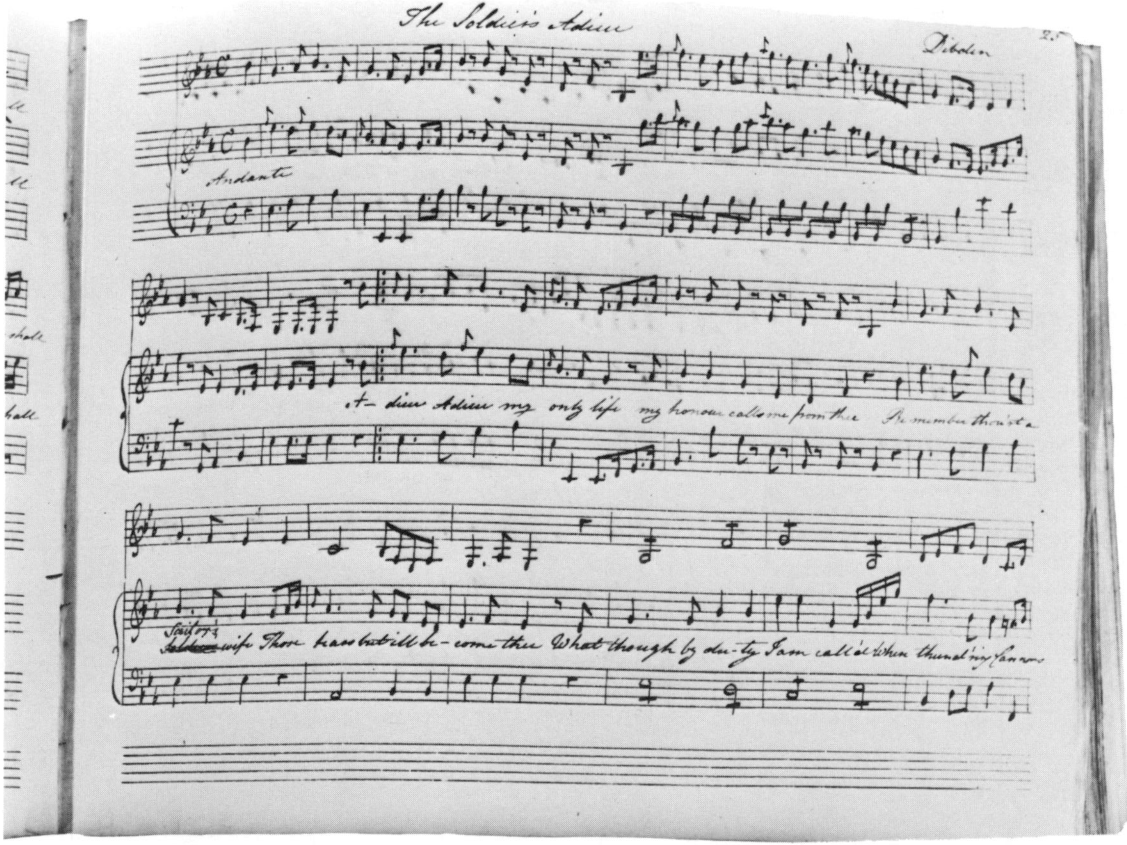

X THE SOLDIER'S ADIEU

ROBIN ADAIR.

(Published at Mitchell's Musical Library & Instrument Warehouse 159 New Bond St: Opposite Clifford St:)

(320)

XI   ROBIN ADAIR

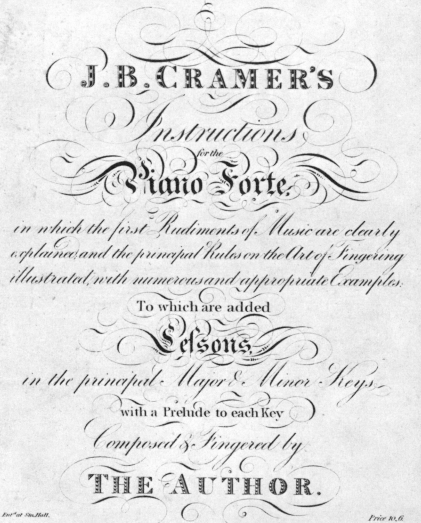

J. B. CRAMER'S
Instructions
for the
Piano Forte.

in which the first Rudiments of Music are clearly
explained, and the principal Rules on the Art of Fingering
illustrated, with numerous and appropriate Examples.

To which are added

Lessons,

in the principal Major & Minor Keys,

with a Prelude to each Key

Composed & Fingered by

THE AUTHOR.

Ent.d at Sta.Hall.   Price 10/6.

London, Printed & Sold by Chappell & C.o Music & Musical Instrument Sellers,124 New Bond Street;
where may be had
All the Works of the above Author.

R & E Williamson Sculp.t

It is the more extraordinary, therefore, that her sister-in-law, Elizabeth, the wife of her brother Edward, should have presumed to criticise adversely Jane's music-copying. In another letter to Cassandra, written on January 8th, 1799, Jane Austen says, not without a touch of acidity,

> Elizabeth is very cruel about my writing music, and, as a punishment for her, I should insist upon always writing out all hers for her in future, if I were not punishing myself at the same time.
>
> *(Letters,* p. 48)

This passage has been taken to mean that Jane Austen had a low opinion of her own powers as a music copyist.[38] If I cannot agree with this interpretation it is because the labour of music-copying is a wearisome and boring occupation to even the most hardened of professional musicians, few of whom, incidentally, have possessed copying hands superior to Jane Austen's. As for Elizabeth's denigration of Jane's writing, it is difficult to believe that it can have been occasioned by any example of her music-copying which has come down to us. Jane's letter may have referred to remarks reported to her by Cassandra, who was then on a visit to the Edward Austens at Godmersham Park, their country mansion in Kent. Cassandra, perhaps, had taken Elizabeth some music which had been copied out by Jane more hurriedly than usual. And yet, even this idea is not wholly convincing, for one feels that Jane Austen would have been particularly careful about any task undertaken to oblige a sister-in-law. Whatever the truth of the matter, we have the evidence of Jane's music manuscripts themselves to prove that Elizabeth's criticism (if it applied to them) was not justified. But before beginning to examine the books in detail it will be worth while to consider briefly the instruments on which their writer actually played the music she troubled to transcribe.

As far as is known, Jane Austen never had the regular use of a grand piano. Indeed, in her earliest years, when she first began to learn music, she probably had to make do, like Catherine Morland, with the 'tinkling' keys of an 'old, forlorn spinnet [*sic*]'. But while still living at Steventon she certainly acquired a more modern instrument, for we know that when the Austens moved to Bath in 1801 everything at Steventon Parsonage was sold, including a pianoforte belonging to Jane. She got eight guineas for it, and she was not disappointed: it was as much as she had hoped for.

It does not appear that a replacement for this pianoforte was among the purchases made for the Austens' new home, for it is not until 1808, when the family, having left Bath after Mr Austen's death in 1806, had moved to Southampton that we find Jane writing to Cassandra, with evident enthusiasm:

> Yes, yes, we *will* have a pianoforte, as good a one as can be got for thirty guineas, and I will practise country dances, that we may have some amusement for our nephews and nieces, when we have the pleasure of their company.
>
> (*Letters*, pp. 243–4)

Thirty guineas was quite a large sum to pay for a square piano in 1808. Cheaper pianos were available, and it is a little surprising that as much could be spared for what was, after all, a luxury. The Austens at that time were very badly off. Mr Austen's death had reduced the income of his widow and daughters to a near-poverty from which they were only relieved by the open-handedness of Mrs Austen's several sons. Jane's personal allowance never exceeded twenty pounds a year (it was only at the end of her life that she earned a few hundred pounds from the sale of her books), and a year or so later (1814) we find her expressing a somewhat 'aunt-ish' disapproval at the proposed purchase of a pianoforte for her recently-married niece, Anna Lefroy:

> I was rather sorry to hear that she *is* to have an Instrument; it seems throwing money away. They will

wish the 24 Gs in the shape of Sheets & Towels six
months hence   (*Letters*, p. 416)

If, as seems likely, Jane Austen was without a pianoforte during her years in Bath, she must have missed the
regular practice hours she had enjoyed at Steventon and
which she was to resume at Chawton. We know, from the
memories of another niece, Caroline Austen, how much
she valued this daily private communion with her
instrument. Writing in 1867, Caroline recalled that her
Aunt Jane

> began her day with music – for which I conclude she
> had a natural taste; as she thus kept it up – tho' she had
> no one to teach; was never induced (as I have heard)
> to play in company; and none of her family cared for it.
> I suppose that she might not trouble them, she chose her
> practising time before breakfast – when she could have
> the room to herself – she practised regularly every
> morning – she played very pretty tunes I thought – I
> liked to stand by her and listen to them; but the music
> (for I knew the books well in after years) would now be
> thought disgracefully easy – much that she played was
> from manuscript, copied out by herself – and so neatly
> and correctly that it was as easy to read as print.

Caroline's appreciation of the fine quality of her aunt's
music-copying is in itself enough to throw suspicion on
Elizabeth's strangely opposite view of it. To us, who have
the good fortune to be able to examine the manuscripts
for ourselves, it is quite clear that Caroline's opinion is to
be preferred to Elizabeth's.

And now let us turn to the Chawton Collection of music
books. It should be said at once that not all the books at
present in the Jane Austen Museum at Chawton originally
belonged to the great novelist herself. One volume of
engraved music was the property of that very sister-in-law,
Elizabeth (née Bridges), who found fault with Jane's
manuscript. Its contents will be considered later. Then
there are two books which are thought to have been com-
piled long before Jane began work on her own music books.

Possibly these were put together by her mother. One of them contains some fairly simple keyboard pieces and a rather larger amount of vocal music. The other, which is marked 'Austen 1778', is almost entirely devoted to songs in English, French and Italian. Though not apparently made by, or even for the immediate use of, Jane herself, there can be no doubt that these books were well known to her and perhaps formed part of her earliest studies of the pianoforte (or harpsichord) and singing. Finally there are Jane's own music books. These may be divided into two categories: the first and most important consists of two volumes of manuscript music, while the second category is of printed music bound up into four volumes, all signed by Jane Austen with, in one case, the contents listed in her own hand.

Elizabeth Bridges' book need not be given detailed scrutiny, though we must pause over one very unusual item – a set of sonatas by a *woman* composer, which is a great rarity in the history of music until the 20th century. Maria Hester Reynolds' 'Sonatas for the Harpsichord or Piano Forte, with an accompaniment for the violin' are decidedly dull (it is unlikely that *they* could ever have sent 'a whole party into raptures'), but the list of those who subscribed to Miss Reynolds' publication is of greater interest. It includes names of some importance in the British musical world of her time, among them Dr Burney, Lady Mount Edgecombe, Master Crotch (an extraordinary infant prodigy) and Mr Shield. There is also a Miss Chard, who might be a connection of Jane Austen's music teacher, Dr Chard.

Maria Reynolds' sonatas are followed by an arrangement of Piccini's overture to his opera, *La buona Figliuola*. We shall find this work again in one of Jane Austen's own music books. The name 'Elizabeth Bridges' is written on this piece and on many other items in the book. It is notable, however, that we never find her married name inscribed there. Though she is known to have sometimes played country dances for her family's amusement in the earliest years of her marriage it is not likely that Elizabeth persevered for long with her music. Probably, like Lady Middleton, she gave it up as soon as her offspring were numerous enough to claim all her attention. Poor woman, she can hardly have done otherwise, for she brought eleven children into the world and failed to survive the arrival of the last of them.

Elizabeth Bridges' music book contains, as well as the pieces already mentioned, the following items: 'Mr Sampieri's Fuga'; The *Battle of Prague*, which is a sonata by a forgotten composer named Kotzwara (we shall meet this naive piece again when we come to examine Jane Austen's own music books); several sets of sonatas by such respectable, if second-grade composers as Gyrowetz and Pleyel (both pupils of Haydn); some sonatas by a much inferior composer named Eichner; three *Sinfonias* with accompaniment for violin and two *cornes de chasse*, by Johann Schobert, and 'Pleyel's celebrated Concertante as performed with the greatest applause at the Pantheon and Hanover Square Concerts, adapted for the Harpsichord or Piano Forte with an accompaniment for the violin'. Though Elizabeth's preoccupation with lying-in will have prevented her from making much use of this book after her marriage it must have been of some interest to Jane Austen during her many visits to Godmersham Park, and it is therefore appropriate that it is now at Chawton among the Austen family's own music books.

At least one of the two music books which may have been the work Mrs Austen, Jane's mother, was probably put together before Jane was born. It contains a few interesting things among much that is trivial. The first two pages are missing, but on pages 3 and 4 we find a march and two minuets by 'Mr Handell', the second minuet being a movement from Handel's overture to his opera, *Arianna*, also known as *Ariadne*. This was one of the most popular pieces of music in 18th century Britain, and it was still in favour after the turn of the century, for it will be recalled that it formed part of the programme of

the concert at the Bath Assembly Rooms which Jane
Austen attended on February 17th, 1805. There are other
pieces by Handel in the book, including an arrangement
of the organ concerto in B flat, written out in full. To copy
such a substantial work must have been a heavy task
for an amateur, and it is the last complete piece, being
followed only by a few experimental scribblings. Apart
from Handel's music, there are songs and duets by Samuel
Howard (1710–1782) and William Boyce (1710–1779).
With one exception, all the songs by Boyce are from his
short opera, *The Chaplet*, first performed in 1749. The
keyboard music includes sets of variations by the Reverend
William Felton, (1713–1769) and little pieces by Hasse and
Arne, and there are numerous light ditties with either
humorous or sentimental words, some of them taken from
the collections of 'Scotch' and 'Irish' airs so popular at
the time. The book bears no date. It contains nothing
which could not have been copied into it before Mrs
Austen's marriage.

The other book which, because it is dated 1778,
appears at first sight to be too early for Jane Austen
herself to have had a hand in its compilation, contains
only two keyboard pieces; otherwise the music is entirely
vocal and is largely culled from that of English composers
(James Hook, John Relfe, William Jackson, Thomas Arne,
William Shield, Thomas Linley, Stephen Storace and
Charles Dibden) and there are also a few pieces by
unnamed composers. The only foreign composers represented are Gluck (*Che faro*, from *Euridici* [*sic*]), Naumann
and Paisiello, though there is also the popular song,
'Since then I'm doomed', better known as '*Je suis Lindor*'
(it was originally composed by Antoine-Laurent Baudron
for Beaumarchais' play, *Le barbier de Seville*) because
Mozart immortalised it by writing a fine set of pianoforte
variations on it. There is, in addition, a song composed to
English words but with music by the Italian composer,
Domenico Corri.

Unlike the first of the two 'pre-Jane' books, the

majority of the pieces in this volume are engraved, though a few of the later items are in manuscript. This raises the question – whose manuscript? Three of the manuscript pieces are from Stephen Storace's opera, *The Siege of Belgrade*, which was brought out at Drury Lane Theatre in 1791. Jane Austen was then sixteen, and it seems far more likely that the Storace songs would have been copied out by her than by her mother, though the manuscript differs in many ways from the clear, elegant writing in the books marked with Jane's own name. Nevertheless, it is possible that the engraved music was bound up in Jane Austen's childhood (in December, 1778, she was three) and that the manuscript pieces were somehow inserted into the book at a later date.

We come now to the books which were Jane Austen's personal property. The three books of engraved pieces contain a good deal of charming, if not particularly 'great' music. It is noteworthy that many of the keyboard works in sonata form are accompanied: subsidiary parts for one or two instruments seem to have been almost *de rigueur* in Jane Austen's youth. There are many such works in this volume. Six Sonatas by the Abbé Sterkel, with violin accompaniment, are followed by six *Quartettos* by Davaux, adapted for the keyboard with an accompaniment for violin and 'tenor' (i.e. viola). Then come two sonatas from Johann Schobert's Op. 3, followed by the Piccini overture, *La buona Figliuola*, adapted for two performers on one keyboard by Thomas Carter. This overture is also in Elizabeth Bridges' collection. Piccini's opera was produced, in English, in London, in 1766, as *The Accomplish'd Maid*. The original libretto, by Goldoni, is distantly based on Richardson's novel, *Pamela*.[39] One wonders if Jane Austen was aware of this fact. She had a high opinion of Richardson. There follow arrangements of five charming overtures to operas by Italian composers. The adaptations, by Ferdinand Bertoni, are for harpsichord or pianoforte with a violin accompaniment, and th first of them, *Medonte*, was composed by Bertoni himself.

The others are *Il Convito*, by Cimarosa (the full title is
Il Convito di Pietra); *Il Trionfo*, by Anfossi; *I Viaggiatori
Felice*, by Piccini, and *Enea e Lavinia*, by Sacchini. Perhaps
because she had seen and liked tham at Godmersham
Park, Jane Austen acquired a copy of the set of Schobert
Sinfonias which are in her sister-in-law's book. Her copy
is to be found in this volume and it is followed by some
keyboard duets: an arrangement of a popular air, 'Shep-
herds I have lost my love', made by J. Billington, a brother-
in-law of the famous singer, Elizabeth Billington; an
excellent *duetto* by Tommaso Giordani, and finally an
oddity – 'Handel's Hallelujah in the Messiah and Grand
Coronation Anthem to which are prefixed two new fugues.
The whole composed and adapted for 2 performers on
one organ or harpsichord by J. March Esqr.'.

Another volume of engraved music, signed on the fly
leaf, 'Miss Jane Austen', contains a set of fourteen Sona-
tinas for the harpsichord or pianoforte, with an accompaniment for the violin, ad libitum, by Ignaz Pleyel. These are
all tiny, technically simple pieces, some in two-movement
and some in variation form. The last is much the most
demanding of the set: it is a theme with five variations
plus a Presto finale which is in fact a sixth variation. Then
comes Pleyel's 'Celebrated Overture', adapted for the
keyboard by T. Haigh. This overture, which is really a
symphony (the terms, as we have seen, were inter-
changeable in much of the 18th century) has several
movements and is quite difficult for an amateur. Its so-
called celebrity was probably no more than a trade
formula to promote sales. If Jane Austen played the 'overture' creditably she must have had more technical proficiency than one had supposed. It is followed by a
concerto by one William Evance, of Durham. There is
little in this music to indicate that it is a concerto rather
than a sonata, though the word 'tutti' appears once in the
first movement. The second movement is a Minuetto and
the finale is a Rondo in which one finds the word 'solo' as
well as 'tutti'. Jane Austen can have had no thought of

playing this concerto with its proper accompaniment for
the accompanying parts (for string quartet) are bound
up with the solo part. William Evance's name has dis-
appeared from musical history. One suspects, despite the
mention of Durham, that he had a Welsh origin. Evance
sounds very like Evans with the hissing sibilance of a
North Wales accent. Was this piece the kind of thing Jane
Austen had in mind when she used the word 'concerto' in
her novels? Hardly, for it is not 'long', and it is certainly
not 'very magnificent', though, in the scene in *Sense and
Sensibility* where Marianne's playing allows Elinor and
Lucy to converse without fear of being overheard,
Jane Austen really meant 'very loud'. The last item in the
book is the once-famous *Battle of Prague* sonata, one of the
earliest of many battle pieces in the history of music.
The subject has rarely proved inspiring to composers:
Beethoven's *Battle of Vittoria* and Tchaikovsky's *1812* are
among the worst compositions by those composers (Liszt's
interesting *Hunnenschlacht* is, perhaps, the exception),
so Kotzwara, the composer of *The Battle of Prague*, need
not be castigated too severely for having produced one of
the crudest and most trivial musical best-sellers of all
time. One regrets that Jane Austen wasted her money
on it, but it seems to have been an indispensable part of
the repertoire of every amateur in her day. The score,
with its running commentary on what the music is supposed to be describing, looks, at first glance, a little like
something by Satie, though it sounds quite otherwise.

One of Jane Austen's volumes of keyboard music is not
a compilation of pieces collected over a period and later
bound together for convenience. At some time in her life,
probably before 1800, she acquired Domenico Corri's
'Select collection of choice music for the Harpsichord or
Piano Forte', which contains twenty-four items, in all of
which Corri had a hand, either as editor, arranger or
composer. Corri, a Roman who went to Scotland in 1771
and later moved to London, was one of the most active of
the many Italian musicians resident in this country. His

daughter married the great pianist-composer, Dussek, with whom he was, for a time, in partnership in the music publishing business. Corri's 'Select Collection' contains a lot of good music: two Haydn Symphonies, numbers 67 and 74, arranged by Corri himself (he calls them over- tures); one of Corelli's concertos; an arrangement of a violin concerto by Giornovichj, or Jarnowick as he was known in England (despite his name, he was a native of Palermo); the overture to Handel's *Occasional Oratorio*; Jomelli's *Chaconne*, once one of the most admired of all orchestral pieces (incidentally it is not a chaconne in form), and many others. Of course there is also much that is ephemeral, including most of the original compositions and variations on popular themes by Corri himself. Jane Austen marked several pieces in such a way as to suggest that she preferred them to, or played them more often than the rest of the collection. These are a Lesson by Kozeluch; Arne's song from *Artaxerxes*, 'The Soldier Tir'd, Arraing'd [*sic*] by Corri'; Schobert's two Lessons, 'March and July' (with accompaniment); and a sonata by Hoffmeister, another composer-publisher who has his own peculiar niche in musical history because of his busi- ness relations with Mozart and Beethoven. The rest of Corri's collection need not be listed, though one is in- trigued by the titles of his own three sonatas, Op. V: *La Bizzara*, *La Disinvolta* and *La Scherzosa*.

The last of Jane Austen's volumes of engraved music contains only solo songs and vocal duets: 'Twelve Can- zonets for two voices' by William Jackson of Exeter; two sets of 'Scots songs for a voice and harpsichord, the music taken from the most genuine sets extant', with words by Allan Ramsey and a flute obbligato to some of them (the insistence on the genuineness of the tunes implies that the manufacturing of fake Scottish melodies to keep pace with the public's insatiable demand for this type of music was already a generally-known fact), and lastly there is 'Colin and Lucy', a 'favorite English ballad, by Mr Tickell, set to music by Signor Giordani'. Richard Tickell was the son-in-law of the composer, Thomas Linley, whose daughter, Mary, he married in 1780. The music was probably written during Giordani's brief sojourn in London, 1781–1783. Though this is the volume whose contents were listed by Jane Austen herself, it will be seen that by her time none of the music in it was new. The canzonets by Jackson had been published in 1780, and Ramsey's words for Scottish songs had been very popular since they were first published, in 1724, as a 'Tea-table Miscellany of Scotch Songs'. It is possible, therefore, that this collection was bound together some time before it came to be regarded as Jane Austen's personal property.

And now for the most interesting and important part of Jane Austen's music library – the two books, one of songs and the other of keyboard music, both carefully written throughout in her own hand. The music paper for the keyboard pieces was bought from Longman & Broderip of Cheapside, a music publishing firm (they also sold instruments) which was in existence from 1778 to 1798. On the front flyleaf is a crudely engraved design featuring an empty scroll in which the purchaser could write what he pleased. The legend it contains reads, 'Juvenile songs and lessons for young beginners who don't know how to practise.' The writing is rather childish, and though the words have the tone of a parent or teacher, they may equally well have been written by a young pupil with an ironic turn of mind who was getting a little tired of hearing that she 'did not know how to practise'. It is a remark frequently made by music teachers. In fact there are no songs in this book, only a varied collection of keyboard pieces, mainly small dances (waltzes, a cotillon, a gigue, a fandango, a strathspey, etc.), marches and sets of variations, including several for four hands on one keyboard· There is not much of greater weight, though there are two sonatas, each containing three movements, one by Mazzinghi (1765–1839) and the other by Steibelt (1765–1823). There is also a long *Pot-pourri* by Steibelt and an arrangement of the overture to Arne's opera, *Artaxerxes*.

Not every piece in the book can be discussed here (not many of them deserve discussion), but some have extramusical interest for us in relation to Jane Austen herself. There is, for instance, early in the collection, a Scottish dance which may have possessed some special significance for a person with Jacobite leanings. Jane Austen, whose sympathies with the Stuart cause are well known, originally wrote above the music some words which she *may* have associated with this tune. The words, in French, are – 'Oh que le Jacobin est bien aimable'. Was there some confusion in her mind between a 'Jacobin' and a 'Jacobite'? The French phrase, however, has been crossed through and replaced with a title, *Mrs. Hamilton of Pincaitlands Strathspey.*

Two of the marches warrant attention. Jane Austen was under the impression that one of them was 'The Duke of York's New March', but in fact the tune is Figaro's song, '*Non Piu andrai*', from Mozart's '*The Marriage of Figaro.*' It had been introduced by Mozart's pupil, Thomas Attwood, into the latter's opera, *The Prisoner*, first heard at Drury Lane in 1792, though *Figaro* itself had to wait until 1812 for a London performance, by which time '*Non piu andrai*', masquerading as a military march, had become extremely popular.[40] It is the only music by Mozart in the Chawton Collection and, not surprisingly, Jane Austen was unaware of its provenance. The other march is by Michael Kelly, principally known in musical history for his connection with Mozart and the Storace family, with whom he was intimate in Vienna before settling in London.

Kelly was an extremely versatile man – a singer-actor-producer-librettist who also 'composed' (with the assistance of trained musicians), which makes him sound rather like an 18th century Noel Coward. He scored a great success at Drury Lane with an opera, *Blue Beard*, put together from music by various composers (this was quite a usual theatrical procedure at that time), but linked by pieces which Kelly claimed as his own.[41] The march from

Blue Beard is one of these, and it is written in Jane Austen's book immediately after the 'Mozart' march. The principal interest for us of Kelly's march lies in the fact that Jane Austen could not have copied it out until shortly before she moved to Bath, for *Blue Beard* was not produced until 1798.

Among the little dances are some waltzes, but it must not be supposed that Jane Austen ever played them as an accompaniment to genuine waltz steps danced by her friends or relations, for in her lifetime the waltz, as a dance, remained taboo in polite English society. These waltzes must be some of the Waltz Country Dances which Mrs Weston played at the dance after the Coles' dinner party, in *Emma*. Two of them are distinguished by the adjective German, and they may be traced to some 'New German Waltzes' published in Preston's *New Country Dances* in 1797.

The more ambitious pieces include a few of some technical difficulty. The sonata by Mazzinghi, which one must suppose Jane Austen to have played since she troubled to copy it out, requires a good, fluent finger technique, while a set of variations on the song, 'My love, she's but a lassie yet', is even more difficult, calling for an ability to play brilliant octave passages, rapid scales and trills, staccato octave scales in C with the third added and passages with crossed hands.

It seems likely that most of the music in this book was copied before 1801. Whether any of it dates from Jane Austen's post-Bath period is difficult to prove, but I would suggest that Steibelt's *10th Pot-pourri*, based as it is on a *Polonaise Russe* and on such airs as Martin y Soler's 'Guardami un poco', which was the rage of St Petersburg in the first years of the 19th century, cannot have been composed before Steibelt's arrival in Russia in 1808. It would, therefore, have been added to the book after Jane Austen had purchased the new pianoforte to which she refers in her letter to Cassandra of 1808, written from Southampton. It is the last piece she copied, but for the overture to

Arne's opera, *Artaxerxes*. As we know, Jane Austen sat
through *Artaxerxes* at Covent Garden in 1814 and derived
little pleasure from it. This was not because she was tired
of it, in the sense of having heard it too often, for we have
no reason to suppose that she had ever heard it before.[42]
Even before hearing it she fully expected it to be 'tiresome',
by which she meant boring. It was the prospect of a whole
evening of singing which she dreaded, and *Artaxerxes*, no
novelty in her day (it had been repeatedly revived since
its first performance in 1762) was that very rare thing in
British Music: an all-sung, full-length opera. Yet Jane
Austen went to the pains of copying out its overture, and
one does not undertake such a task without a strong motive.
She must have liked the piece, and it is just possible that
her decision to add it to her collection (it is the final item
in the book) was the direct result of hearing it played at
Covent Garden.

I have left until last the book which seems to me to be
the most interesting of all, not because of the intrinsic
value of the music, but because it contains a few pieces
which must intrigue all readers who delight in Jane
Austen's works and in such facts as are known about their
author. It is almost entirely devoted to songs and duets
(Jane Austen always spells it 'duetts') and is written
throughout in her most clear and elegant hand (*Plate
IX*).

There is only one page of keyboard music, marked
simply, *Airs de Ballets de la Caravane*, without any composer's name. In fact the music is from Grétry's opera,
La Caravane de Caire, which scored a success in its time
mainly because of its spectacular ballets. A song, '*Sous un
berceau de Jasmin*', which comes a little later in the book,
is from the same source.

The first piece in the book is an incomplete extract
from what seems to be one of the numerous 'Turkish' or
'Harem' operas of the period, since it is an aria, "'Tis in
vain', sung by a character called Zaida. The heroines
of such works, the most famous examples of which are

Mozart's operas *Zaide* and *Die Entfuhrung aus dem Serail,* were usually called Zaida or some such variant of the name as Zobieda or Zorayda.[43]

''Tis in vain' is followed by a little song, the music of which is by Haydn, who would, however, have been surprised and probably not amused to find a truncated version of the first movement of his Sonata in C, Hob. XVI/ 35, transformed into a comic ditty called 'William'. Jane Austen did not always give the names of the composers of the songs she chose (though she did mention Haydn in connection with 'William'), but it soon becomes clear that she preferred the home-grown product, for most of them are by such composers as Calcott, Shield, Arnold (extracts from his opera, *The Mountaineers*) and above all Dibden. Dibden was at the height of his fame in Jane Austen's lifetime and she shows a decided preference for his work, though the air, 'Go and my truth', which she ascribed to him, has been credited to an Italian composer named Vento.[44] As Dibden made use of Vento's air in his own opera, *Lionel and Clarissa,* Jane's mistake was perfectly natural. Jane Austen wrote out at least seven songs by Dibden and possibly more, for some anonymous pieces, as yet untraced to their sources, are quite in his style.

In an essay of this size it is not possible to discuss all the thirty-six songs in the book, but there are some which demand more attention than others. First among these is a song by Dibden called 'The Soldier's Adieu'. It is the words, not the music of this song which must amuse all admirers of Jane Austen, and even then it is not so much Dibden's words (he usually wrote the texts as well as the music of his songs) which are interesting as a significant alteration to them made by Jane Austen. The song begins:

> 'Adieu, Adieu my only life
> My honour calls me from thee –
> Remember thou't a soldier's wife
> Those tears but ill become thee.'

and this is how Jane Austen wrote it, and, perhaps for some time sang it, until one day she seized her pen, drew a careful line through the word 'soldier's', and substituted for it, 'Sailor's' (*Plate* X). Thus Miss Jane Austen, the creator of dashing Captain Wentworth, refined Captain Harville, soulful Captain Benwicke, bluff Admiral Croft and manly young Lieutenant Price. And thus Miss Jane Austen, the proud sister of two gallant sailor brothers.

There are several French songs in the book and among them is a *Duo du Roi Theodore*, '*Filles charmantes, jeunes amants.*' This is actually taken from an Italian opera, *Il Re Teodoro*, by Paisiello. Why both words and title should have been written by Jane Austen in French is a little puzzling, unless her cousin Eliza (née Hancock), Comtesse de Feuillide, afterwards to marry Jane's brother Henry *en secondes noces*, was concerned in the business. Eliza might have introduced her to some of the other French songs, including a *Chanson Bearnaise*, of which only the melody is given; an air, '*La danse n'est pas ce que j'aime*', from Grétry's opera *Richard Coeur de Lion*, and perhaps even to the *Marseillaise*, which Jane Austen calls 'The Marseilles March'. There is also an unaccompanied Italian song, an *Arietta Veneziano*, '*La Biondina in gondoletta*', which is the tune used long afterwards by Liszt for his piano piece, *Gondoliera*. According to Liszt, it is by a certain Cavaliere Peruchini.

Storace has been mentioned already. The book contains several pieces by him – more, indeed, than at first appears, though he is named as the composer of the 'duett', 'O Plighted Faith'. His name is not given, however, as the composer of two songs which come later in the book, though he wrote them both.[45] The first is 'Captivity', which is about the imprisonment of Queen Marie-Antoinette. It was written in 1792, while Marie-Antoinette still languished in prison. A few months later Storace wrote another song, this time a 'Lamentation of Marie-Antoinette, late Queen of France, on the morning of her execution'. Jane Austen not only copied out both these songs, but as in the case of Dibden's 'Soldier's Adieu', she made a slight but important alteration to the second of them. Forgetting all about poor Marie-Antoinette, she renamed the song, 'Queen Mary's Lamentation'.[46] Knowing, as we do, of her, perhaps [semi-humorous, adherence to the Stuart cause and of her romantic attachment (more genuine, one feels) to the memory of the ill-fated Mary Queen of Scots it is easy to understand her reason for doing so. Here were two songs, written in an expressive contemporary idiom, with which, by the simple substitution of Mary for Marie, she could fancy herself to be lamenting the tragic fate of her favourite historical character.

The last song in the book is called *The Match Girl*. It may come as a surprise to some readers (it did to me) to discover that matches had been invented in Jane Austen's time. I had supposed, until I saw this song, that the lighting of candles in those days involved the use of some less sophisticated form of ignition. But the first lines of the song, 'Come buy of poor May good matches', proves otherwise. The composer of the song is not named but, in view of the match girl's name, one hopes that he was called Bryant.

It would be idle to pretend that many of the songs and piano pieces which Jane Austen copied with such care and labour into her books are of a good musical standard. Indeed, some pieces suggest that from a musical point of view she was a little lacking in that very quality which, on the evidence of her novels, she most approved in her Anne Elliot and deplored the lack of in her Mary Bennet – the quality she called 'taste'. 'Taste' is not very evident in her choice of music, too many of the items in her collection being no more than superficially pretty and sometimes rather worse than that, though, to be fair, one must allow that third-rate music, if it preponderates, does not form the whole of her music library. We may be disconcerted by, and critical of the absence of music by such composers as Mozart and Beethoven (whose works, however, were not easy to come by in the England of Jane Austen's time), but we must remember that she did own pieces by other great composers, among them Handel, Haydn and Gluck.

And she cannot be blamed for ignoring J. S. Bach, for, like most of her contemporaries, the name Bach would have meant for her Johann Christian – the 'London' Bach – and not Johann Sebastian, who had yet to be 'discovered'. If the Chawton Collection were all that we know of Jane Austen's music library we might well be surprised that it does not contain anything by such a leading figure of eighteenth century London musical life as Johann Christian Bach, whose popular sonatas were said to be 'such as ladies can execute with little trouble'. Even more surprising would be the absence of music by his successors, Muzio Clementi and, above all, J. B. Cramer, who is the only composer actually named in any of the Austen novels. As will be seen, however, works by all these composers are to be found among the many interesting items in the Second Collection.

It has not yet been sufficiently emphasised that much, perhaps most of the vocal music in the Chawton volumes is of theatrical origin. Music proliferated in the English theatre of the eighteenth century, and though serious, full-length, all-sung opera had little chance after *The Beggars' Opera* (1728) had ousted Italian opera from popular favour (the unique success of *Artaxerxes*, written to an English translation of an Italian libretto, was not to be repeated for many years), the audiences of the day still demanded a lot of music in their theatrical entertainments. Short operas of less than an hour's duration, known as 'after-pieces', were produced in quantity, and many of the songs and duets in the Austen books come from works of this type by Shield, Arnold, Dibdin, etc. These tunes were often the 'pop' songs of their day, and their lasting qualities have, in many instances, proved stronger than the popular music of later periods. This is natural enough, for most of them are either the work of highly professional musicians or are based upon the time-tested Celtic airs which, as we have seen, were in the forefront of musical fashion in the eighteenth and nineteenth centuries.

CHAPTER XI

Jane Austen's Music-Books:
The Second Collection

THOUGH the volumes in this collection seem at first sight to be of less importance than those of the Chawton Collection their contents reveal that they are of great interest and value to Austen scholars.

It is true that none of them bears Jane Austen's signature (as do several of those at Chawton) but it is by no means impossible that some of the manuscript music is in her hand, and there is every reason to believe that the two volumes marked with Cassandra Austen's name consist of items, both printed and in manuscript, which once belonged to Jane Austen. The Austen Papers contain no hint that Cassandra was at all musical; in fact, there is a family tradition that, like Elinor Dashwood, she was quite the reverse. Why then do two thick volumes in this collection bear her name? The answer seems to be that the books in question contain that part of Jane Austen's music library which, remaining unbound at the time of her death, was subsequently bound up on the instructions of her sister.

As well as the two books signed by Cassandra Austen, the Second Collection includes four interesting volumes of music which once belonged to Jane's sister-in-law, Mrs Henry Austen. Austen scholars are agreed that this lady, who was, of course, Jane's glamorous cousin, Eliza Hancock, later the Comtesse de Feuillide and eventually the wife of Jane's favourite brother Henry, played quite an important role in Jane's early life and may have provided her with material for her art. Austen authorities still argue as to whether Eliza Hancock, whose letters reveal her to have been flirtatious, worldy and decidedly frivolous, served as a model, in some aspects, for the cold-hearted Lady Susan and subsequently for Mary Crawford. As a very young girl, Jane was able to watch the devastating effect of her brilliant cousin's charms on the Austen boys. First James Austen, the eldest brother, was ensnared and later Jane's beloved brother Henry was 'taken in'. Eliza certainly must have possessed much of Mary Crawford's fascination (it should not be forgotten that she was Henry's senior by some ten years), but her music books reveal something else which she had in common with the anti-heroine of *Mansfield Park*: she played the harp. She probably played the piano as well and she certainly sang (two of her music books are devoted to vocal works, all in manuscript), but it is her ability to play a 'harp as elegant as herself' which will be triumphantly seized upon by those Austen scholars who believe her to have been the model for that mixture of charm, kindheartedness and gaiety with worldliness, materialism and subservience to fashion which makes up the interesting but flawed personality of the harp-playing Mary Crawford.

One of Eliza's two volumes of harp music may have been acquired while she was the Comtesse de Feuillide, for it is a printed collection called *Feuilles de Terpsichore, ou journal: composé d'Ouvertures, d'Airs arrangés et d'Airs avec accompagnement. Pour la Harpe*, and it was printed in Paris.

The other volume is a more varied selection of pieces. It includes several duets for harp and pianoforte (such duets were performed at the Henry Austens' musical party at their Sloane Street house in 1811) by various leading composers – Dussek, Steibelt, Fiorello, etc. – as well as piano solos by Cramer, Corri, Griffin (one of the numerous infant prodigies of the day) and many others, most of whom are now totally forgotten. There are also ten waltzes by Steibelt with obbligato parts for the tambourine, a type of 'duet' made popular by this composer and his young English wife, whose possession (according to Grove's Dictionary) of 'considerable personal attractions', as well as abilities as a percussionist, helped to promote the success of this fashionable musician's London concerts.

Eliza's collection of harp music leads one to wonder about the fate of her harp after her untimely death in 1813. Did it become the property of Henry Austen's niece, Fanny Austen Knight? It will be recalled that Fanny was in London in 1815, staying with her Uncle Henry in Hans Place and taking harp lessons three times a week from a Mr Meyer (Jane Austen called him Meyers), whose unpunctuality and tendency to give short measure gave rise to Jane Austen's strictures, already quoted, on music masters who, she maintained, were 'made of too much consequence'.

Eliza Austen's two books of vocal music, which include glees and catches as well as numerous songs and arias, are entirely in manuscript. They form a remarkably representative list of the composers popular in eighteenth century London, ranging from such great masters as Purcell, Handel, Haydn and Mozart (we find there an air from *The Magic Flute*) to the minor Italian composers of the day (Marchesi, Anfossi, etc.) and native song writers like Dibdin, Shield and Linley.

One of the books, signed and dated by Eliza Austen on August 19th, 1799, some twenty months after her marriage to Henry, includes many songs with obbligato parts for a violin, and some in a kind of full score, that is, with additional parts for viola and bass. Curiously enough, there is not a single song by a Frenchman to be found among the forty-odd composers represented. This suggests that Eliza left behind her most of the music she acquired during her years in France when she returned hurriedly to England in 1783 to escape the dangers of the French Revolution.

Interesting as are Eliza Austen's music books, they are naturally of less importance than the two 'Cassandra Austen' books, since the latter, as we have seen, almost certainly formed a part of Jane Austen's own music library. Someone, probably Cassandra, very sensibly arranged the printed and manuscript music into separate volumes, though, perhaps by a mistake of the binder, a printed copy of a Clementi sonata is the first item in the volume otherwise devoted to the manuscript music – manuscript for which several hands appear to be responsible. In this book, which is marked C. E. Austen, some of the work is obviously not that of Jane Austen herself, but there is some which resembles her authentic music writing, notably a clear and elegant copy of a complete Haydn sonata.

The Clementi Sonata, Op. 26, which begins the collection (unfortunately one of that composer's weakest effusions) dates from 1791. It bears the composer's autograph, and one would like to know the circumstances which allowed Clementi to sign the Austen's copy of his work. Clementi was a very learned and original master, but one would never know it from this sonata, and still less from the manuscript copies of three Waltzes with tambourine accompaniment which follow – mere trivia which show that this most astute of business men among composers was not above 'cashing in' on Steibelt's success with similar ephemera. Presumably Jane Austen acquired these waltzes for use when dance music was needed for the amusement of her nieces and nephews, one of whom perhaps obliged with a tambourine or a triangle (Clementi allows the use of both).

An ornamental version of the national anthem follows – actually an extract from a concerto by J. C. Bach which introduces it as a theme for variations – and then an anonymous 'Lesson' in F and a Minuet with variations which uses the tenor clef for some of the left hand part (could Jane Austen read the tenor clef? It begins to seem likely that she could). Next comes the Haydn sonata above mentioned, the one in C, Hob. XVI/35 – the very sonata whose first movement is the origin of the humorous song, 'William', which Jane Austen copied into one of the Chawton Collection of music books. A copy of Piccini's Overture, *La Buona Figliuola*, marked 'Mrs Austen' (there are other copies of this once popular piece in the Austen music books), and a Lesson in C by 'Mr Jones' (probably Richard Jones, who published a collection of such lessons in 1776) follow, and then several pieces, including a complete three-movement sonata, by unnamed composers. An Air with Variations in B flat by a M. Blattman Defuille brings us to a collection of vocal music for one, two and occasionally three voices, among which we find a certain amount of good music, including three of Haydn's *English Canzonets* and several charming songs by Arne.

The most entertaining of the vocal pieces, however, are among the two small collections of nursery rhymes, set for two voices and piano. These pretty and amusing little songs were revived and performed with considerable success at concerts during the Jane Austen Bicentenary Celebrations of 1976. But, as might be expected, the majority of the vocal items consists of the popular 'national' songs of the day – Irish, Scottish and Italian for the most part (there is even a 'Hindoo Girl's Song' by a Mrs Curwen), plus a few sentimental drawing-room duets whose composers' names are never stated. Interspersed among these simple tunes are a few more instrumental pieces of which the most notable are an elaborate and difficult *Musette Variée* by Louis von Esch and a curious piece scored for horns and clarinets with pianoforte and entitled 'Music from the oratory while the ghost appears'. The music is actually a part of Jomelli's once celebrated Chaconne which, adapted by Michael Kelly for his successful musical drama, 'The Castle Spectre', became associated in the public mind with the most effective scene in that play, a scene, moreover, which established a long-lasting fashion for stage ghosts. There is also a French air, *On ne savoit trop embellir*, with variations by Matthias von Holst, but about this composer there will be something to say in the discussion of the final book in the Second Collection, a substantial volume of printed music for the pianoforte bearing the full signature of Cassandra Elizabeth Austen.

Devoted exclusively to instrumental music, this final

volume begins, appropriately enough, with a modest pianoforte tutor called *Instructions and Lessons for Learners* by J. Jasse, exactly the sort of publication which might have been used by Dr Chard for the earliest stages of his pupils' studies. There follows a major work by one of the great figures of the eighteenth century London musical world: a set of *Six Sonatas for the Harpsichord or Piano Forte, with an accompaniment for the violin,* by Johann Christian Bach, his first name here anglicised to John. Bach was one of the many sons of the great Johann Sebastian, and in his lifetime a much more famous figure than his father. After the Bach sonatas come several sonatas by less celebrated composers. There is, for example, a so-called 'Favorite' [*sic*] Sonata by a certain Zwingmann, autographed by its composer, and there are two sonatas by a British pupil of Haydn's named Thomas Haigh. Like many other such works in the Austen Music Books, these Haigh sonatas have a simple violin accompaniment and they pander to public taste by the introduction of 'Scotch Airs'. Scotch Airs are similarly woven into *Three Grand Sonatas* by Ignaz Pleyel (another Haydn pupil) which, having accompaniments for both violin and violoncello, are, in effect, Trios.

We now come to the important name of Cramer, a composer whose music is notably absent from the main Chawton Collection. It will be recalled that some of Cramer's music was sent down from Highbury with the Broadwood pianoforte by Frank Churchill, and before I had the good fortune to be able to investigate the Second Collection I was surprised by the lack of any music by Cramer in the music at Chawton. I concluded that the Chawton books probably did not represent the whole of Jane Austen's music library. Some of Cramer's compositions and possibly some by other leading composers of the time, such as Clementi, must, I felt sure, have been lost, perhaps because they had not been preserved by binding. While I was partly right in my conjectures, we now know that Cassandra *did* arrange for the rest of the

Austen sheet music to be bound. As a consequence, we possess visible proof that Jane's repertoire did indeed include some of Cramer's music and also some of Clementi's.

The two works by Cramer which are in this volume are (a) a sonata into which is introduced *God Save the King*, and (b) a set of variations on another popular air, *Dulce Domun*. They are both very far from being among Cramer's better works, but for want of anything superior we must suppose that this was the sort of music which Jane Austen had in mind when she introduced Cramer's name into *Emma*. What Jane Fairfax thought of it can be imagined: as the possessor of admirable musical 'taste' she cannot have approved of Frank Churchill's choice, though she will have kept her opinion of it to herself, knowing that he meant very well and that (as he himself observed to Emma) the sending of the music with the pianoforte was an act prompted by 'true affection'.

A few light salon pieces by Louis von Esch and two sets of variations on popular airs, one of them by Dr Arnold on a theme of Mozart, bring us to another item which is of some interest in connection with *Emma*. It always seemed to me curious that Jane Fairfax should have chosen to demonstrate the powers of her new instrument by playing a very undemanding little Irish air, *Robin Adair* (recte *Eileen Aroon*). She probably played better things as well, but this tune and 'one of the waltzes that were danced at Weymouth' are the only items in her 'recital' actually named by Jane Austen. While it is true that *Robin Adair* may have been played because it had a symbolic meaning for Jane and Frank, it was, nevertheless, a curious choice for such an accomplished pianist . . . unless what Jane Austen *really* had in mind was an elaborate set of variations on the theme by George Kiallmark (*Plate* XI) which forms the next item in the volume under discussion. This piece must have been known to Jane Austen, and it is therefore highly likely that she meant her 'second lead' heroine to be playing Kiallmark's variations rather than some simple, unadorned version of *Robin Adair*. The variations are, in fact, quite charming as music and highly pianistic.

There are many other sets of variations and arrangements of popular tunes by Dussek, Woelfl, Mazzinghi and other minor composers resident in London in the Regency period – too many for all of them to be listed here. We may, however, mention *Gary Owen, a favorite* [sic] *dance (performed by Mr Weippart) in the new pantomine Harlequin Amulet, arranged as a rondo for the Piano Forte by Mr Latour*. Mr Weippart was, of course, the celebrated harpist who was among the 'hirelings' whose performance gave so much satisfaction at Mrs Henry Austen's party in 1811. Jane Austen wrote to Cassandra that his name was new to her. Perhaps she had not noticed, or had forgotten that it appeared on the title page of *Gary Owen*, though she might have acquired the piece later.

Another 'favorite melody' by Mozart, this time an air from *The Magic Flute*, with variations by R. Burbidge, confirms that Jane Austen was at least aware of Mozart's existence (and we know that she heard a Mozart 'Overture' in Bath), though she seems to have known nothing of his original piano music.

Much of the later part of the volume consists of dances, including several reels and numerous dance tunes extracted from successful theatre pieces of the time and arranged by various hack musicians then working in England. Among these pieces is *The Celebrated Fairy Dance, arranged as a Rondo by Matthias von Holst*, whose name we have already met in one of Eliza Austen's volumes. Von Holst, a native of Courland who arrived in England in 1807, is, as the great-grandfather of the great British composer, Gustav Holst, a figure of some interest in the history of music.

The volume ends with two little collections of dance music in arrangements by James Dale, one 'with instructions for figures in dancing', the other with tunes which include 'the new Waltz'.

Intermingled with these inevitably trivial publications are a few more serious (though not very serious) compotitions: yet one more sonata with violin *obligé*, this time by J. A. Adam; *The Favorite Overture to 'The Bedouins or Arabs of the Desert'*, by Sir A. Stevenson, Mus. Doc. (something of a curiosity), and last, but far from least, one of the greatest successes of the day: Steibelt's *Grand Concerto*, Op. 33, which, with its *Adagio* based on a 'Scotch Air' (then considered a sure-fire sales promotion ingredient – Steibelt used *Annie Laurie*), and its celebrated *Storm Rondo*, made its composer's name famous throughout Europe. That Jane Austen played the technically demanding *Rondo*, or anyway tried to do so, is indicated by the pencilled fingering which has been applied to some of its passage-work. Part of the impression made by Steibelt's 'Storm' was the shock effect produced by its unusually large volume of sound. The composer himself, not satisfied with the tone of the pianos of the time, arranged for a second piano, hidden in the orchestra, to double his part at the first performance, but one grand pianoforte would have been effective enough in a drawing-room. I had long suspected that this work might have been the 'very magnificent' concerto which Marianne played in the Middletons' drawing-room while Elinor and Lucy Steele launched their barbed exchanges under cover of its 'noise', and its presence in one of the 'Cassandra Austen' Music Books – a copy, moreover, which has been used for study – goes some way towards proving my suspicion to be well-founded. Apart from the mild little work by William Evance in one of the books of the Chawton Collection, it is the only full-length 'modern' concerto in any of the Austen Music Books.

In spite of her own claim, made with almost a touch of bravado and probably with semi-humorous intent, that she did not really care for music, and in spite of the variable 'taste' to be observed in her choice of songs and pianoforte pieces, Jane Austen was certainly more musical than she sometimes chose to allow. One does not study an instrument, practise it daily and devote precious hours to music-copying without a very strong impulse from within. She was typical of many amateurs in that she liked, above all things, to play what she already knew well, evidently finding it more satisfying to run through the pieces she had learned as a girl than to struggle with the technical difficulties of new music. Nevertheless, her solitary hours at the keyboard, though they may have been musically unadventurous, were very valuable to her as a relaxation, and if, as has been conjectured, they may have acted as some kind of 'trigger' for her imagination, helping her to organise and plan her material before committing it to paper,[47] then their place in her life as an artist has a special significance, and the question of *what* she played becomes of much less importance than the fact that the very act of playing contributed something to her greatness as a writer.

SELECT BIBLIOGRAPHY

For Jane Austen's *Novels, Letters* and *Minor Works*, the Oxford Edition. Edited by R. W. Chapman.

My Aunt Jane Austen. A Memoir. By Caroline Mary Craven Austen. Spottiswoode, Ballantyne, 1952.

Biographical Notice [by Henry Austen]: in *The Novels,* Vol. V (*Emma*).

A Memoir of Jane Austen. By James Edward Austen-Leigh. Richard Bentley, 1870.

Jane Austen: Her Life and Letters. By W. and R. A. Austen-Leigh. Smith Elder, 1913.

Presenting Miss Jane Austen. By May Lamberton Becker. G. G. Harrap, 1953.

Jane Austen & her Predecessors. By Frank W. Bradbrook. C.U.P., 1966.

Jane Austen, Facts & Problems. By R. W. Chapman. O.U.P., 1948.

Jane Austen, the Six Novels. By W. A. Craik. Methuen, 1965.

Jane Austen. By Yasmine Gooneratne. C.U.P., 1970.

Jane Austen. Bicentenary Essays. Edited by John Halperin. C.U.P., 1975.

The Double Life of Jane Austen. By Jane Aiken Hodge. Hodder & Stoughton, 1972.

Jane Austen. By Elizabeth Jenkins. Gollancz, 1958.

Talking of Jane Austen. By Sheila Kaye-Smith & G. B. Stern. Cassell, 1943.

Jane Austen and Her Art. By Mary Lascelles. O.U.P., 1939.

Jane Austen and Her World. By Marghanita Laski. Thames & Hudson, 1969.

The Novels of Jane Austen. By Robert Liddell. Longman, 1963.

Jane Austen's English. By K. C. Phillips. André Deutsch, 1970.

Dear Jane: A Biographical Study of Jane Austen. By Constance Pilgrim. William Kimber, 1971.

Jane Austen and her Music Books. By Mollie Sands. Jane Austen Society, Report for 1926.

Before Jane Austen. By Harrison R. Steeves. Allen & Unwin, 1966.

Critical Essays on Jane Austen. By B. C. Southam. Routledge & Kegan Paul, 1968.

Jane Austen's Literary Manuscripts. By B. C. Southam. O.U.P., 1964.

Jane Austen. The Critical Heritage. By B. C. Southam. Routledge & Kegan Paul, 1968.

NOTES

1 Ballroom dances in Jane Austen's day were danced in what were called sets. A set was formed when several couples ranged themselves in lines, the gentlemen facing the ladies. The dancers took turns to perform the elaborate figures in the centre lane. A general movement of the dancers between the figures brought each couple in turn to the top of the set. It was a social distinction to lead out a set for the first dance of a ball. Fanny Price is characteristically dismayed to find herself distinguished in this way at the ball in *Mansfield Park*. Emma Woodhouse, on the other hand, accustomed to lead, is somewhat crestfallen to discover that she is expected to give place to Mrs Elton (according to old Mr Woodhouse, a newly-married bride is always the first in company) at the Westons' ball at the Crown Inn.

2 Frank Bradbrook. *Jane Austen and her Predecessors*, Chapter 3, *The Picturesque*.

3 But the charming drawing of their niece, Fanny Knight, which is sometimes attributed to Jane Austen, is really by her sister Cassandra.

4 William Chard was a native of Winchester, but before his appointment as deputy cathedral organist in that city he had been a chorister at St Paul's Cathedral in London. He seems to have been a lively, convivial character, fond of hunting and, at least in his later years, not over-zealous about the strict observance of his duties as Master of the Music at Winchester College (in 1818 he was reprimanded for neglecting them, though he appears to have escaped censure as cathedral organist and choirmaster). Like many of the clergy of his day, he was a 'pluralist', for he also held the organistship of St Maurice's Church in Winchester. His prominence in Winchester society must have been considerable: he was elected a Freeman of the city as early as 1797, made a Justice of the Peace in 1811 and for a short period (1832–35) he even donned the chain of office of Winchester's mayoralty – surely an unusual distinction for a cathedral organist.

5   This piece was almost certainly by Handel, whose over-
    ture to his Italian opera, *Arianna*, known in England as
    Ariadne remained immensely popular for upwards of
    sixty years. One movement from this overture – the
    Minuet – appears in the Austen family's manuscript
    music books.

6   *Jane Austen's Letters*. Introduction, p. xl.

7   Dr Chapman, in his edition of Jane Austen's letters,
    acknowledges his indebtedness to Mr Archibald Jacob for
    detailed information about the five glees mentioned in this
    letter. 'Strike the harp in praise of Bragela' is the third
    line of Henry Bishop's chorus, 'Strike the harp in praise of
    my love'. The other vocal pieces mentioned are 'In peace
    love tunes the shepherd's reed': a glee by J. Attwood;
    'Rosabelle', 'The Red Cross Knight', and 'The May Fly',
    all glees by J. W. Calcott.
        The term 'Lesson' originally meant a piece of a purely
    educational nature, but later it was often loosely applied
    to any kind of solo instrumental composition, though it is a
    little unusual to find it used in this way as late as 1811.
    Jane Austen's letters contain another mention of Lessons:
    writing to her sister on September 16th, 1813, she said –
    'Fanny desires me to tell Martha with her kind love that
    Birchall assured her there was no 2nd set of Hook's
    Lessons for Beginners – & that by my advice, she has there-
    fore chosen her a set by another Composer'. Robert Birchall
    owned a long-established music publishing business in
    New Bond Street. James Hook's *Lessons for Beginners* are
    still in use.

8   Jane Austen was being strictly accurate when she wrote
    that it was the *name* Wiepart [*sic*] which 'seemed' famous,
    for the Weipparts had been known as musicians for many
    years. Johann (later John) Erhardt Weippart, a native of
    Schweinfurt, in Franconia, born in 1766, emigrated to
    England and established himself in London where he
    made a great reputation as a harpist, playing frequently at
    Covent Garden and Drury Lane Theatres. His younger
    brother, Johann (John) Michael, born in 1775, also emi-
    grated to England at about the same time and made a

name for himself as a fine harpist and harp teacher. Both brothers played several instruments. John Michael eventually dropped his first name, probably to avoid confusion with his brother. Dr Chapman's edition of Jane Austen's letters contains a note, giving the name of M. Weippart as the harpist who played at Mrs Henry Austen's party, but as both brothers were alive and working in London in 1811, and as John Erhardt was the more famous of the two, it cannot be quite certain which was the Weippart in question. The Weippart brothers were elected members of the Royal Society of Musicians, John Erhardt in 1797 and John Michael in 1806.

9   Constance Wright. *Louise, Queen of Prussia* (1970). Pp 93–4, 241.

10   Catherine Stephens, 1784–1882. Cf. *Grove's Dictionary of Music & Musicians*.

11   Dr Chapman's note (*Jane Austen's Letters:* Letter No. 93, p. 384) about *Artaxerxes* describes it as an 'Italian Opera' without mentioning the composer's name. Thomas Arne's *Artaxerxes* was set to his own translation of Metastasio's original Italian text.

12   In 1839 she married the octogenarian Earl of Essex and was widowed a year later. This sounds like a calculated risk which paid off.

13   He is said to have introduced the stethoscope into British medical practice, though the instrument was invented by R. T. H. Laënnec in 1816.

14   Quoted by Lord Brabourne (*Letters of Jane Austen*, ed. Edward, Lord Brabourne) from the diary of his mother, Lady Knatchbull (née Fanny Knight).

15   Robert Liddell. *The Novels of Jane Austen*. P. 62.

16   R. W. Chapman. *Jane Austen, Facts and Problems*. Pp. 49–50.

17   B. C. Southam. *Jane Austen's Literary Manuscripts*. P. 45.

18   Though most modern editions of Jane Austen's novels print all her references to pianofortes as a single word and without an accent, the early editions were almost as

inconsistent in this matter as the authoress. For example, Dr Chapman's edition of *Sense and Sensibility*, based on the second edition, which was revised by Jane Austen herself, gives 'pianoforte' on p. 26; pianoforté on p. 83, and pianoforté on p. 144.

19 C. B. Southam. *Jane Austen's Literary Manuscripts*. P. 74.

20 Gertrud Schmeling, the daughter of a poor musician of Cassel, was born in 1749. The story of her childhood makes dreadful reading. Her mother died soon after Gertrud was born and her father formed the habit of tying the child up when he went out to work. This treatment resulted in a serious spinal weakness which troubled her to the end of her long life.

A natural musician, little Gertrud secretly taught herself the rudiments of violin playing. Her father, when he discovered what she had been doing, was very angry, and beat her for it; but then he saw that she might have talents which could be economically valuable, and indeed she had: after intensive training the child developed a remarkable technique and was soon exhibited in public. This brought her to the notice of the English ambassador in Vienna, and on his advice the Schemlings moved to London, where Gertrud was at once taken up by High Society and even patronised by the queen. However, her noble patronesses considered the violin to be an unfeminine instrument, and as Gertrud already possessed a strong, clear voice they undertook to have her trained as a singer. She made her début at Dresden in a opera by Hasse and was an instant success, but much sorrow and tribulation still lay before her. She was engaged by King Frederick II of Prussia for his Royal Opera Company, and treated by him with characteristically ruthless tyranny (on one occasion she was dragged from her bed by soldiers and forced to sing in spite of indisposition). She was also forbidden to marry. Nevertheless, she did marry a French violoncellist named Mara – and soon lived to regret it. Eventually Madame Mara escaped both her husband's and her employer's ill treatment, and in the years that followed she made enormous sums of money and achieved great celebrity, particularly in England. When Catherine Morland heard her in Bath she must have been past her prime, and three years later she left England for Russia, settling in Moscow in 1802, where she began a new career as a teacher. But even now her troubles were not over, for the Napoleonic invasion of 1812 and the burning of Moscow left her entirely ruined, and she had to fly for her life.

The unfortunate woman, now in her mid-sixties, went to Revel, in what was then called Livonia, and began to rebuild her teaching connection. It would have been as well had she been content to remain there for the rest of her days, but at the age of seventy she was seized with the extraordinary idea of reappearing as a singer in London, the scene of her former triumphs. Somehow she obtained an engagement at the King's Theatre; she appeared on the stage, opened her mouth to sing – and no sound emerged from it. Poor Mara! This was her last, disastrous public appearance. However, she lived on to the age of eighty-four and was honoured by Goethe, who sent her a flattering poem on her eighty-first birthday.

21 The wheel has turned full circle. Sheet music is, once again, extremely expensive and often in short supply. Laborious hand-copying is, however, no longer necessary, for a wide range of relatively cheap photographic processes makes instant duplication available to most people. Though often illegal, this practice is now so widespread as to constitute a danger to the whole future of the music publishing industry.

22 See page 36.

23 Robert Liddell. *The Novels of Jane Austen.* P. 94.

24 K. C. Phillips. *Jane Austen's English.* P. 88.

25 Sheila Kaye-Smith and G. B. Stern. *Talking of Jane Austen.* P. 130.

26 Cecil J. Sharp & A. P. Oppé. *The Dance. An historical survey of Dancing in Europe.* 1924. Pp 29–30.

27 Dr Chapman's edition of *Emma* (1923) gives facsimiles of pages from T. Wilson's *Analysis of Country Dancing* (published 1811), one of which mentions 'The Brunswick Waltz'. But Dr Chapman abstained from all comment on the subject of dancing (see Appendices to *Emma*, p. 507).

28 Jean Rousseau (not to be confused with Jean Jacques Rousseau). *Traité de la Viole* (1687).

29 Jane Austen's letters include references to Miss Allen, Miss Bell, Miss Cleves and Miss Ann Sharp, governesses all. Miss Sharp was a particularly close friend.

30 Now Camden Terrace.

31 Dr Chapman's researches have revealed that 'Molland's' was a pastry-cook's, though I have seen it described elsewhere as a shoe shop.

32 It seems very probable that T. Cooke was Thomas Simpson Cooke, a native of Dublin who had been born in 1782. He was an infant prodigy, and a favourite pupil of Giordani. Cooke played several instruments with considerable skill and he also composed much. About 1812 he suddenly blossomed forth as a singer, with such success that he removed to London in 1813, where he remained as principal tenor at the Drury Lane Theatre for twenty years. He was well known as a composer of glees, and a glee by T. Cooke was sung from the manuscript at Loder's concert on February 22nd, 1815.

33 Henry Field gained considerable fame in later life and was known in England as 'Field of Bath', to distinguish him from his internationally celebrated namesake, John Field ('Russian Field').

34 The fact that Thomas Field was to play the timpani at Loder's concert was one of the few details mentioned in the *Bath Chronicle* advertisement, though not in that of the *Bath Journal*.

35 The following notice appeared in a Bristol paper in 1821: Died, March 15th, 1821, Alexander Herschel, Esq., well-known to the public of Bath and Bristol as a performer and elegant musician; and who for forty-seven

years was the admiration of the frequenters of concerts and theatres of both those cities, as principal violoncello. To the extraordinary merits of Mr Herschel was united considerable acquirement in the superior branches of mechanics and philosophy, and his affinity to his brother, Sir William Herschel, the illustrious astronomer, was not less in science than in blood. To a large circle of professional friends the uniform gentlemanly manners of Mr Herschel rendered him at once an object of their warmest regard and respect.

36 The rejected chapter of *Persuasion* may be found in the Chapman edition of *The Novels of Jane Austen*, Volume V.

37 See J. B. Priestley. *The Prince of Pleasure and his Regency*. 1969. P. 85.

38 Mollie Sands. Jane Austen and her Music Books. Address to the Jane Austen Society, 1956.

39 Roger Fiske. *English Theatre Music in the 18th Century*. P. 325.

40 Ibid., pp. 518–519.

41 Ibid., pp. 572–574.

42 Ibid., p. 310: and Jane Austen's Letters, ed. R. W. Chapman. Letter No. 93, p. 384.

43 Ibid., pp. 378–380.

44 Ibid., p. 605.

45 Ibid., p. 441.

46 In a letter to her sister, dated Feb. 8th, 1807, Jane Austen wrote: 'It is no use to lament. – I never heard that even Queen Mary's Lamentation did her any good, & I could not therefore expect benefit from mine' (*Letters*, p. 176). She knew that Cassandra would smile at her allusion to Storace's song.

47 Jane Aiken Hodge. *The Double Life of Jane Austen*. Pp. 113, 133.

INDEX

Abbey Mill Farm, 74
Accomplish'd Maid, The, (opera libretto), 143
Adam, J. A. (Sonata by), 163
Agricultural Reports, The, 74
Allen, Miss, 172
Allen, Mr, 39
Allen, Mrs, 39, 40
Anfossi, Pasquale, 144, 157
——, *Il Trionfo* (opera), 157
Annie Laurie (Scottish air), 163
Arne, Dr Thomas, 8, 24, 142, 169
——, *Artaxerxes* (opera), 8, 24, 25, 150, 154, 169
——, Overture to *Artaxerxes*, 147
——, *The Soldier Tir'd* (song from *Artaxerxes*), 146
——, Songs (various), 159
Arnold, Dr A., 151, 154, 161
——, *The Mountaineers* (opera), 151
——, *Variations on a theme by Mozart*, 161
Ashe, Andrew, 123, 124, 129
Ashe, Mrs (née Comer), 124, 125, 129
Attwood, Thomas (*The Prisoner*, opera by), 148
Austen, Caroline (niece of J.A.), 28, 29, 30, 46, 139
Austen, Cassandra (sister of J.A.), xi, 4, 8, 20, 23, 24, 26–28, 106, 137, 138, 149, 155, 157–160, 162, 163, 167, 173
Austen, Edward, afterwards Knight (brother of J.A.), 20, 21, 27, 29, 137

Austen, Elizabeth (née Hancock, later de Feullide, wife of Henry Austen), 8, 22, 23, 26, 116, 152, 155–157, 162
Austen, George (nephew of J.A.), 131
Austen, Rev. George (father of J.A.), 138
Austen, Henry (brother of J.A.), 8, 22, 24, 26, 28, 64, 152, 156, 157
Austen, James (brother of J.A.), 23, 131, 156
Austen, Mrs (mother of J.A.), 28, 138, 141, 142
Austen Papers, The, 155
Austen-Leigh, J. E., 6

B., Lady (Lady Bridges), 21
Bach, C. P. E. (*Essay on the True Art of Playing Keyboard Instruments* by), 96
Bach, J. C., 20, 57, 154, 158, 160
——, *La Clemenza di Scipione* (opera), 20
——, *6 Sonatas*, 160
Bach, J. S., 154
Baly-craig, 101
Barton, 47
Barton Cottage, 44, 46
Basingstoke, 17
Bates, Miss, 51, 81, 82, 87, 91, 92, 98, 101, 102, 105, 107, 108
Bates, Mrs, 78, 82, 84, 86, 87, 97, 101
Bath, 1, 17, 19, 20, 39, 40, 103, 113, 121, 125–127, 138, 139, 149

175

Heywood, *Charlotte*, 37
Highbury, 77–79, 81, 84, 88, 89,
102, 105, 107, 109, 110, 160
Hofmannsthal, Hugo Von, 62
Hoffmeister (*Sonata for piano forte*
by), 146
Holder, Miss, 21, 22
Holst, Gustav, 162
Hook, James, 142, 168
——, *Lessons for Beginners*, 168
Howard, Samuel, 142
Hurst, Mrs, 54
Inchbald, Mrs (*Lovers' Vows*, play
by), 72
Invetto, Signor, 18
Irish Ascendency, 77
Irish Sea, 100
Italy, 20

Jackson, John, 8
Jackson, William, 142, 146
——, *12 Canzonets for two voices*,
146, 147
Jane Austen Memorial Trust
Museum at Chawton, 131, 139
Jane Austen Bicentenary
Celebrations, 159
Jarnowick (Giornovichj), 146
Jasse, J. (*Pianoforte Tutor* by), 160
Jenkinson, Mrs, 58, 59
Jennings, Mrs, 2, 36, 48
Johnson, Dr Samuel, 4, 94
——, *Dictionary*, 95
Johnson, Mrs, 36
Jomelli, Nicola, 146
——, *Chaconne*, 146, 159
Jones, Richard (*Lessons* by), 159

Kaillmark, George (*Variations on
Robin Adair* by), 132, 161, 162
Kalbrenner, Frederick, 124

Kelly, Michael, 148, 149
——, *Blue Beard* (opera), 148, 149
——, *The Castle Spectre* (play with
music), 159
Kellynch Hall (or Kellynch-hall),
113, 117
Kellynch Lodge, 121
Kent, 20, 137
Kentish Gazette, The, 21
Knight (or Austen-Knight),
Elizabeth (née Bridges), 137,
139–141
Knight (or Austen-Knight),
Fanny, 25, 27, 28, 30, 37, 117,
157, 167
Knightly, Mr, 78, 80, 83, 88,
90–92, 101, 102, 108, 109
Knightly, John, 3
Knightly, Isabella (née *Woodhouse*),
106
Kotzwara (*The Battle of Prague*,
Harpsichord Sonata by), 141,
145
Kozeluch (*Lesson* for
Harpsichord), 146
Krumpholtz, 24
King's Theatre, London, 20, 129

L., Mrs, 28
Lady Susan, 31, 35, 57, 74, 156
Latour, Mr (*Gary Owen*, arranged
by), 162
Lee, Miss, 66, 106
Lefroy, Anna (née Austen), 23,
24, 138
Lesley Castle, 32, 33, 35, 36
Lessons, 24, 168
Liddell, Prof. Robert, 31, 108,
171
Linley, Mary, 147
Linley, Thomas, 142, 147, 157